Conduct Disorders in Childhood and Adolescence

DEVELOPMENTAL CLINICAL PSYCHOLOGY AND PSYCHIATRY SERIES

Series Editor: **Alan E. Kazdin**

In the Series:

1 CHILD DEVELOPMENT AND PSYCHOPATHOLOGY
Donna M. Gelfand and Lizette Peterson

2 CHILD AND ADOLESCENT PSYCHOPHARMACOLOGY
Magda Campbell, Wayne H. Green, and Stephen I. Deutsch

3 ASSESSMENT AND TAXONOMY OF CHILD AND ADOLESCENT PSYCHOPATHOLOGY
Thomas M. Achenbach

4 INFANT PSYCHIATRY: AN INTRODUCTORY TEXTBOOK
Klaus Minde and Regina Minde

5 SUICIDE AND ATTEMPTED SUICIDE AMONG CHILDREN AND ADOLESCENTS
Keith Hawton

6 PSYCHOPATHOLOGY AMONG MENTALLY RETARDED CHILDREN AND ADOLESCENTS
Johnny L. Matson and Cynthia L. Frame

7 HYPERKINETIC CHILDREN: A NEUROPSYCHOSOCIAL APPROACH
C. Keith Conners and Karen C. Wells

8 LIFE EVENTS AS STRESSORS IN CHILDHOOD AND ADOLESCENCE
James H. Johnson

9 CONDUCT DISORDERS IN CHILDHOOD AND ADOLESCENCE
Alan E. Kazdin

Forthcoming:

TEMPERAMENT AND CHILDHOOD PSYCHOPATHOLOGY
William T. Garrison and Felton Earls

Conduct Disorders in Childhood and Adolescence

Alan E. Kazdin

Developmental Clinical Psychology and Psychiatry 9

Conduct Disorders in Childhood and Adolescence

Alan E. Kazdin

Volume 9.
Developmental Clinical Psychology and Psychiatry

To Karen M. Conamor

For information address:

SAGE Publications, Inc.
2111 West Hillcrest Drive
Newbury Park, California 91320

SAGE Publications Inc.
275 South Beverly Drive
Beverly Hills
California 90212

SAGE Publications Ltd.
28 Banner Street
London EC1Y 8QE
England

SAGE PUBLICATIONS India Pvt. Ltd.
M-32 Market
Greater Kailash I
New Delhi 110 048 India

Printed in the United States of America

Library of Congress Cataloging-in-Publication Data

Main entry under title:

Kazdin, Alan E.
Conduct disorders in childhood and adolescence.

(Developmental clinical psychology and psychiatry series ; v. 8)
Bibliography: p.
Includes index.
1. Child psychopathology. I. Title. II. Series:
Developmental clinical psychology and psychiatry ; v. 8.
[DNLM: 1. Child Behavior Disorders. W1 DE997NC v. 8 /
WS 350.6 K23C]
RJ499.K37 1986 618.92'89 86-1818
ISBN 0-8039-2750-9
ISBN 0-8039-2751-7 (pbk.)

SECOND PRINTING, 1988

CONTENTS

SERIES EDITOR'S INTRODUCTION

Interest in child development and adjustment is by no means new. Yet only recently has the study of children profited from advances in both clinical and scientific research. Advances in the social and biological sciences, the emergence of disciplines and subdisciplines that focus exclusively on childhood and adolescence, and greater appreciation of the impact of such influences as the family, peers, and school have helped accelerate research on developmental psychopathology. Apart from interest in the study of child development and adjustment for its own sake, the need to address clinical problems of adulthood naturally draws one to investigate precursors in childhood and adolescence.

Within a relatively brief period, research on psychopathology of children and adolescents has evolved considerably. Several different professional journals, annual book series, and handbooks devoted entirely to the study of children and adolescents and their adjustment document the proliferation of work in the field. Nevertheless, there is a paucity of resource material that presents information in an authoritative, systematic, and disseminable fashion. There is a need within the field to present the latest developments and to represent different disciplines, approaches, and conceptual views to the topics of childhood adjustment and maladjustment.

The Sage series on *Developmental Clinical Psychology and Psychiatry* is designed to serve uniquely several needs of the field. The series encompasses individual monographs prepared by researchers in the fields of clinical psychology, psychiatry, and related disciplines. The primary focus is on developmental psychopathology, which here refers to the diagnosis, assessment, treatment, and prevention of problems of children and adolescents. The scope of the series is necessarily broad because of the working assumption that understanding, identifying, and treating problems of youth cannot be resolved by narrow, single-discipline, and parochial conceptual views. Thus, the series draws upon multiple disciplines and diverse views within a given discipline.

The task for individual contributors is to present the latest theory and research on various topics including specific types of dysfunction, diagnostic and treatment approaches, and special problem areas that affect adjustment. Core topics within clinical work are addressed by the series. The present monograph focuses on conduct disorder and serious antisocial behavior such as aggressive acts, theft, vandalism, firesetting, and related behaviors in children and adolescents. The nature and scope of the problem as well as its prevalence and costs to society make antisocial behavior one of the most socially significant mental health problems. This book integrates current findings on description, diagnosis, assessment, treatment, and prevention of conduct disorder. In addition, new models to approach the investigation and treatment of antisocial behavior are identified to guide future research.

—*Alan E. Kazdin, Ph.D.*
Series Editor

PREFACE

Conduct disorder refers to a clinical problem among children and adolescents that encompasses aggressive acts, theft, vandalism, firesetting, running away, truancy, defying authority, and other behaviors referred to as "antisocial." Many antisocial behaviors, in mild form, emerge over the course of normal development and hence prove to be of little consequence. Persistent and extreme patterns of these behaviors among children and adolescents reflect a serious clinical problem with broad personal and social impact. These more extreme patterns are delineated here as conduct disorder.

The significance of conduct disorder stems in part from the fact that it constitutes one of the most frequent bases for referral of children and adolescents for psychological and psychiatric treatment. Children with severe antisocial behavior are not only seriously impaired as youths but also are likely to manifest psychiatric problems, criminal behavior, and social maladjustment when they become adults. The problem does not end when antisocial youths reach adulthood; as parents, they are likely to pass along antisocial behaviors to their children, who continue the cycle.

The significance of the clinical and social problem that conduct disorder reflects is heightened by the absence of solutions. At present, no clearly effective strategies to treat or prevent antisocial behavior have been identified. Although research continues to explore treatment options, antisocial behavior continues as one of the most costly of childhood disorders. Children and adolescents and their families utilize multiple social services and are in frequent contact with the mental health and criminal justice systems. There are as well the personal costs to the many victims of aggressive, violent, and cruel acts completed by conduct-disordered youths. Such youths are victims themselves given the abuse, neglect, and poor care to which they are often subject.

This book describes the nature of conduct disorder and what is currently known from the research and clinical work. Findings are drawn from such areas as epidemiology, psychology, psychiatry, and child development. The subject matter brings us to such topics as psychiatric diagnosis, child-rearing practices, parent psychopathology, the contributions and interactions of heredity and environment, psychotherapy research, and others. The book considers core areas of work that occupy current research efforts. These include elaboration of alternative approaches to diagnose and to assess conduct disorder, identification of the factors that place children at risk for engaging in seriously antisocial behavior and continuing such behavior as adults, and current methods of treating and preventing antisocial behavior. The purpose is to provide a comprehensive yet concise view of conduct disorder in children and adolescents and to point to new areas of work. To that end, the book ends by outlining four new models and approaches to critical questions regarding diagnosis and treatment of antisocial youths.

I am indebted to several colleagues, both in my own department at the University of Pittsburgh School of Medicine and at other institutions, who have shared their work and time for preparation of the present monograph. The support of a Research Scientist Development Award (MH00353) has been central to my development and understanding of childhood dysfunction. Grants (MH35408, MH39642, MH39976) from the National Institute of Mental Health and from the Rivendell Foundation to investigate characteristics, course, and treatment of conduct disorder were provided during the period in which this book was prepared. It is a pleasure to acknowledge my colleagues in these projects, David Kolko, Karen Marchione, and Larry Michelson, as well as the sources of support for this work.

Several individuals warrant special mention because of their help in seeing this monograph to its final form. Lollie Phillips and Claudia Wolfson helped prepare the manuscript and supporting materials. Nicole Kazdin, my 13-year-old daughter, edited selected chapters and gave her candid opinions about the overall merit and interest value of the book. (We decided to publish the book anyway.) Michelle Kazdin, my 7-year-old daughter, helped in checking the final version of the manuscript and in providing early-morning pauses to enliven my spirit.

—A.E.K.

1

INTRODUCTION AND NATURE OF THE PROBLEM

Antisocial behaviors include a broad range of activities, such as aggressive acts, theft, vandalism, firesetting, lying, truancy, and running away. Although these behaviors are diverse, they are usually considered together. The main reason is that the behaviors in fact often go together. Thus, children who are very aggressive are likely to show some of the other antisocial behaviors as well. In addition, the behaviors all violate major social rules and expectations; many of them also reflect actions against the environment, including both persons and property.

Many different terms have been applied to denote antisocial behaviors including acting out, externalizing behaviors, conduct disorder or conduct problems, and delinquency. Two of the terms are worth delineating at the outset. For present purposes, *antisocial behavior* will be used to refer broadly to any behaviors that reflect social rule violations and/or that are acts against others. In this usage, antisocial behaviors refer to various acts such as fighting, lying, and other behaviors whether or not they are necessarily severe. Such behaviors are evident in clinically referred youths, but they also are seen in varying degrees in most children over the course of normal development.

The term *"conduct disorder"* will be used to refer to instances when the children or adolescents evince a *pattern* of antisocial behavior, when there is *significant impairment* in everyday functioning at home or school, or when the behaviors are *regarded as unmanageable by significant others*. Thus, conduct disorder is reserved here for antisocial behavior that is clinically significant and clearly beyond the realm of normal functioning.[1] Clinically severe antisocial behavior is likely to bring the youth into contact with various social agencies. Mental health services (clinics, hospitals) and the criminal justice system (police, courts) are the major sources of contact for youths whose behaviors are identified as severe. Within the educational system, special services, teachers, and classes are often provided to manage such children on a daily basis. Even though the behavioral problems that constitute conduct disorder are familiar, it is useful to illustrate the level of severity and the surrounding circumstances that characterize clinically severe levels of impairment.

TWO CASE ILLUSTRATIONS

Greg

Greg is a 10-year-old boy who lives at home with his mother, father, two younger brothers, and a baby sister. He was a troublesome child who was referred to an outpatient clinic because of his excessive fighting, temper tantrums, and disruptive behavior at home and at school. At home he argued with his mother, initiated fights with his siblings, took money from his parents, and constantly threatened to set fires when his parents disciplined him. On three separate occasions he had set fires to rugs, bedspreads, and trash in his home. One of these fires led to major damage costing several thousand dollars. He also lied frequently; at school his lying got others into trouble which precipitated frequent fights with peers and his denial of any wrongdoing.

Greg was brought to the clinic because his parents felt he was becoming totally unmanageable. A few incidents in particular were mentioned as unusually dangerous such as his attempt to suffocate his 2-year-old brother by holding a pillow over his face. Also, Greg has recently begun to wander the streets at night and to break windows of parked cars. Because of some of the older boys with whom he interacts in the neighborhood, his parents are also worried that he will become a "hood." Greg's parents occasionally resorted to severe punishment by using paddles and belts or by locking him in his room for 2-3-day periods. These occasions appear to have been in response to firesetting in the home.

Several characteristics of Greg's family life are noteworthy. Because Greg's mother and father have worked for all of Greg's life, a relative, usually the maternal grandmother, has had primary care responsibility of the children. For the two years before Greg was brought for treatment, his father had been employed only sporadically. The father spent much of his time at home sleeping or watching television. The loss of work, income, and lack of his help around the house contributed to increased stress at home. Greg had said that he could not stand to be with his dad because he got mad all the time for little things. The mother worked full-time and tried to manage the home as well. However, she was not at home very much. The mother has a history of major depressive disorders as well as two suicide attempts within the last three years. She was hospitalized on each occasion for approximately two months. Greg's behavior at home and at school have been purported to be worse than usual during these periods.

At school, Greg was in the fourth grade. His intelligence was within the normal range (full-scale IQ score of 96 on the Wechsler Intelligence Scale for Children-Revised [WISC-R]). His academic performance was behind grade level and he was in a special class because of his disruptive behavior. His teacher reported that he is overactive and disruptive in class. His parents were told that unless they seek psychological consultation, he will not be allowed to return to the school next year.

Greg had been in treatment when he was younger. When he was 6 years old, he was seen by his pediatrician for his uncontrollable behavior at home and at school. At that time, he was given stimulant medication to control his overactivity. The mother reports that the medication did not help and after about six months she discontinued its use. The parents brought Greg to an outpatient treatment center for evaluation. They felt that Greg's behavior became more serious at home and at school and that they did not know where to turn. They talked about giving him up or putting him in a special boarding school where more discipline might make him shape up.

Ann-Lee

Ann-Lee is a 13-year-old girl who, until recently, has lived with her mother and stepfather and her 9-year-old brother. For the last 6 months, she was living in a youth shelter under the custody of the courts because of repeatedly running away from home. The shelter placement was temporary pending completion of a court-ordered psychiatric evaluation. Ann-Lee was hospitalized for a brief period to complete this evaluation.

Ann-Lee was reported by her parents to be oppositional, argumentative, and to lie and steal often. Her stealing has been the most prominent symptom. She stole clothes and jewelry from the homes of relatives and friends as well as from her parents. In fact, her parents locked their bedroom door and all dresser drawers to protect their valuables. She stole small items from department and discount stores but this was much less frequent than stealing from other persons.

Running away has been a major problem as well. Over the past three years, Ann-Lee has run away from home on four separate occasions. Each time, the police had to be called. Running away has been precipitated by her being grounded for stealing or cigarette smoking at home. When she was grounded, she was made to remain in her room. She usually escaped, even though her room was on the second floor of her home. On the last occasion when she escaped and ran away, she was gone for three nights. The police found her wandering the streets late at night on the other side of town (about 10 miles from her home). She would not tell them who she was or where she lived. Consequently, several hours elapsed before she was returned home.

When Ann-Lee was 5, her mother and father were divorced. During this year (kindergarten), Ann-Lee had great difficulty at school in terms of following instructions and making friends. According to her mother, this period marked the beginning of her antisocial behavior. Ann-Lee's school difficulties continued and teachers complained about her problems in completing school work. Her mother moved to a new area. In the new school, Ann-Lee did satisfactory school work and remained at grade level. Teachers said she was smart enough to do well (WISC-R full scale IQ = 105) but she had a bad attitude and poor motivation. She is currently in the eighth grade where she gets Bs, Cs, and Ds in her academic subjects.

Although behavioral problems were evident throughout Ann-Lee's history, in the last three years they increased in severity and frequency. At this time, a custody dispute began between her mother and biological father. The dispute began when the father was denied access to the children for one summer because of his excessive drinking. The father occasionally would take Ann-Lee and her brother to bars, where he stayed for several hours and drank. When the custody battle began, tension increased for all family members. As part of the fighting, Ann-Lee falsely accused her stepfather of child abuse. This increased efforts of her biological father to obtain custody and also led to a formal investigation of the stepfather. All charges of abuse were eventually dropped. The strain on relations associated with the custody and abuse battle, according to the parents, seemed to precipitate the most recent incident of Ann-Lee's running away and was associated with increases in her argumentativeness and unmanageability.

Ann-Lee was admitted to an acute care psychiatric hospital for an evaluation. Hospitalization also provided the opportunity to explore the family resources and problems more fully. The goal of the evaluation was to recommend to the court an appropriate placement for her, to explore the possibilities of treatment, and to help accelerate resolution of the custody dispute. Eventually, Ann-Lee was placed into a foster home and brought to a clinic for individual psychotherapy.

General Comments

These two cases were presented to illustrate the type and severity of problems that conduct disorder represents. The cases underscore a few important points. First, in each case, the child engaged in rather severe behaviors. The problems were not merely failing to comply with parental requests, getting into arguments with siblings, engaging in temper tantrums, and not completing homework from school. These latter sorts of behaviors were present in each case but did not serve as the primary basis for seeking professional attention.

Second, the parents felt that the child was out of control and that their own resources for coping were exhausted. In one case, the school helped to precipitate treatment by making return of the child contingent on seeking professional help. Third, the parents had their own problems and sources of stress including in these cases, marital discord, a history of significant psychiatric dysfunction, and unemployment. In one case, three other children were in the home and parents expressed the difficulties in raising a problem child with others to attend. Finally, and most obviously, the cases involved several agencies on behalf of the child including the school, the courts, mental health facilities, and a youth service center. Conduct-disordered youths often are in contact with multiple social services.

CLINICAL AND SOCIAL SIGNIFICANCE

The case descriptions illustrate at a personal level some of the problems that conduct disorder represents and the unfortunate circumstances with which it may be associated. Multiplied many times and with broader diversity than two cases can reflect, the personal and social consequences are enormous. The significance of conduct disorder can be punctuated by highlighting a few characteristics of the problem, briefly now, and in more detail in subsequent chapters.

• *Prevalence.* The prevalence of conduct disorder is difficult to estimate given very different definitions that have been used and variations in rates for children of different ages, sex, socioeconomic class, and geographical locale. Estimates of the rate of conduct disorder among children have ranged from approximately 4% to 10% (Rutter, Cox, Tupling, Berger, & Yule, 1975; Rutter, Tizard, & Whitmore, 1970).

When rates are evaluated for specific behaviors that comprise conduct disorder and youths themselves report on their activities, the prevalence rates are extraordinarily high. For example, among youths (ages 13-18) more than: 50% admit to theft; 35% admit to assault; 45% admit to property destruction; and 60% admit to engaging in more than one type of antisocial behavior such as aggressiveness, drug abuse, arson, vandalism (see Feldman, Caplinger, & Wodarski, 1983; Williams & Gold, 1972). Even though it is difficult to pinpoint how many children might be defined as conduct disorder at a particular age, data consistently reveal that the problem is great by most definitions.

• *Clinical Referrals.* Another measure of the scope of the problem is the extent to which referrals to clinical services include antisocial behavior. Estimates have indicated that referrals to outpatient clinics for aggressiveness, conduct problems, and antisocial behaviors encompass from one-third to one-half of all child and adolescent cases (Gilbert, 1957; Herbert, 1978; Robins, 1981).

• *Stability of the Problem.* Among childhood disorders, antisocial behavior tends to be relatively stable over time (Beach & Laird, 1968

Robins, 1978). The stability departs from many other disorders that often are age specific and remit over the course of development. Thus, when children evince consistent antisocial behavior such as aggressive acts toward others, it is unlikely that they will simply grow out of it.

• *Prognosis.* It follows from the stability of the behavior that the prognosis is likely to be poor. In fact, conduct problems in childhood and adolescence portend later problems in adulthood including criminal behavior, alcoholism, antisocial personality (i.e., continued conduct disorder), other diagnosable psychiatric disorders, and poor work, marital, and occupational adjustment (Robins, 1966; Wolfgang, Figlio, & Sellin, 1972).

• *Transmission Across Generations.* Antisocial behavior is not only stable over time *within individuals* but also *within families.* Antisocial behavior in childhood predicts similar behaviors in one's children (Huesmann, Eron, Lefkowitz, & Walder, 1984; Robins, 1981). The continuity is evident across multiple generations. Grandchildren are more likely to show antisocial behaviors if their grandparents have a history of these behaviors (Glueck & Glueck, 1968).

• *Costs to Society.* Antisocial behavior has been identified as one of the most costly of mental disorders to society (Robins, 1981). The reason is that a large proportion of antisocial youths remain in continued contact with mental health and criminal justice systems well into adulthood. The expense is more concretely conveyed by identifying specific examples of antisocial behavior among juveniles. In the mid-1970s, separate estimates of the costs of vandalism and firesetting among juveniles in the United States were approximately $600 and $700 million, respectively in a *single* year (*Fire in the United States,* 1978; United States Senate Judiciary Committee, 1976). The costs for psychiatric and psychological treatment, family social work, juvenile adjudication and incarceration, special programs in education, and by social agencies would be difficult to estimate. That they are exhorbitant is beyond any reasonable doubt.

• *Absence of Effective Interventions.* The significance of conduct disorder is heightened by the absence of clearly effective interventions.

Several treatments have been implemented for antisocial behavior including diverse forms of individual and group therapy, behavior therapy, residential treatment, pharmacotherapy, psychosurgery, and a variety of innovative community-based treatments (Kazdin, 1985; McCord, 1982; O'Donnell, 1985; Shamsie, 1981). At present no treatment has been demonstrated to ameliorate conduct disorder and to controvert the poor prognosis alluded to above.

Even with only a brief sketch, it is evident that conduct disorder in children and adolescents represents a major social problem. A discussion of the nature and scope of the social problem neglects the personal tragedy that antisocial behavior reflects. There is, of course, the chronic maladjustment and unhappiness of those whose conduct is of clinically severe proportions. In addition, there are the many victims of acts of murder, rape, robbery, arson, drunk driving, and spouse or child abuse, which are carried out to a much greater extent by persons with a history of antisocial behavior than by other persons. Because of the many victims, antisocial behavior plays a role unlike that of many other psychiatric problems (e.g., psychoses) that receive center stage attention in research on the mental disorders.

DEFINING AND IDENTIFYING ANTISOCIAL BEHAVIOR

Given the case illustrations above and the types of behaviors that are involved, there should be little difficulty in identifying antisocial acts and the persons who perform them. In fact, not all antisocial behavior comes to the attention of parents, teachers, and professionals who are involved in clinical and legal agencies. Many antisocial behaviors are not attended to or identified as worthy of treatment or professional attention. There are a number of considerations that are relevant for identifying conduct disorder.

Normal Behavior as the Backdrop for Evaluation

Many antisocial behaviors emerge in some form over the course of normal development. Thus, the significance and special characteristics of conduct disorder as a clinical problem must be viewed against the backdrop of normal development. Several studies have examined the emergence of antisocial behaviors and their patterns of change over the course of development. The results have indicated surprisingly high prevalence rates for behaviors among samples of normal children and adolescents.

For example, in the longitudinal study by MacFarlane, Allen, and Honzik (1954), mothers reported on the problems of their normal children from early childhood through early adolescence (from under 2 through 14 years of age). Among the many noteworthy findings was the relatively high prevalence of specific antisocial behaviors. For example, at age 6, lying was reported as a problem for the majority (53%) of boys. Yet by age 12, the percentage had dropped considerably (to about 10%). For girls, the pattern was more dramatic with a rate of lying reported as a problem at age 6 (approximately 48%) and none reported as a problem after age 11.

Similarly, Achenbach and Edelbrock (1981) completed a cross-sectional study of children from 4 to 16 years old and reported high rates of specific antisocial behaviors. For example, disobedience at home and destroying one's own things were reported as problems by the parents for approximately 50% and 26% of normal 4- and 5-year-old children. For 16-year-old adolescents, the rates for these behaviors dropped to approximately 20% and 0%, respectively.

Several other studies have shown that many antisocial behaviors are relatively frequent at different points in normal development (Crowther, Bond, & Rolf, 1981; Jessor & Jessor, 1977; Lapouse & Monk, 1958). The specific rates for selected behaviors are not easily identified because individual studies have utilized different definitions of the behaviors of interest and different methods of assessing them. Yet across the different studies, the pattern has been relatively consistent. The presence of antisocial behavior is relatively common at different points in normal development. In addition, these antisocial behaviors typically decline over the course of development. Because most children do not show conduct disorder when they mature, early antisocial behavior is not necessarily clinically significant. On the other hand, relatively high rates of antisocial behavior and continued performance rather than a decline of these behaviors represent a clinically significant departure from the normal pattern (cf. Patterson, 1982).

Consideration of antisocial behavior as part of normal development also requires mention of sex differences in these behaviors. Among normally functioning children, boys generally have been found to engage more frequently in stealing, fighting, truancy, destructiveness, and lying over the course of development (MacFarlane et al., 1954; Rutter et al., 1970; Werry & Quay, 1971). In general, boys tend to show higher levels of "acting out" (externalizing) types of symptoms such as those characteristic of antisocial behavior. In contrast, girls tend to show greater prevalence for "neurotic" (internalizing) types of symptoms such as shyness, hypersensitivity, and physical complaints.

Even though many antisocial behaviors decline with age for most normal boys and girls, the behaviors are also relatively stable. Stability in this context refers to the correlation of behavior of children assessed on two or more occasions (e.g., a few years apart). The correlation reflects the extent to which children retain their relative standing for the behaviors in their peer group. A high correlation suggests that persons identified as relatively aggressive at one age are also relatively aggressive at a later age. Several longitudinal studies of aggressive behavior with youths ranging in age from 2-18 years have found considerable stability of aggressive behavior up to 21 years later (see Olweus, 1979).

In general, the identification of serious antisocial behavior requires consideration of developmental norms. Among normal samples, antisocial behaviors vary as a function of age and sex. Looking for the presence of fighting, stealing, or other behaviors is not enough to decide that a clinical problem exists.

Characteristics of the Behaviors

Many characteristics of the behaviors themselves determine whether clinical levels of severity are evident. *Frequency and intensity of the behaviors* are central features that determine whether the child is identified as clinically impaired. Obviously, the extent to which a child frequently engages in such behaviors as fighting, stealing, and lying, determines whether the behavior warrants attention.

Many antisocial acts are low-frequency, high-intensity behaviors. Their significance stems from the magnitude of their consequences when the behavior occurs rather than the actual frequency of the behavior. These are also behaviors that are more severe or extreme relative to variations one might see in the course of normal development. For example, firesetting may be brought to the attention of clinical and legal agencies because the child has set "only" one or two fires. Similarly, highly dangerous acts of aggression against others such as attempting to injure a sibling or parent with a weapon or torturing and killing of a pet can serve as a basis for seeking treatment. In such cases, the behaviors are obviously extreme relative to their counterparts in everyday life (e.g., arguments and minor physical fighting between siblings, teasing a pet).

Repetitiveness and chronicity of the acts also help to define clinical levels of antisocial behavior. One instance of the behavior alone may not bring the child to the attention of others. Repetition of the act and a protracted history of continuing the behavior over time and settings imbue the behaviors with much greater significance. Persistent antisocial behavior reflects the fact that the usual ministrations of parents, teachers, and peers and unspecified maturational processes have not had their desired impact.

Breadth of antisocial behaviors is also important in defining deviance. Antisocial behaviors come in "packages" or constellations. Children who perform one type of antisocial behavior are likely to perform others as well. For persons who refer children to treatment, the behaviors may be subsumed by a single rubric such as unmanageability or acting out behaviors. Yet, the many different ways in which a child is unmanageable contributes to whether the child is referred to clinical services.

The dimensions highlighted here are considered in combination in the process of identifying clinically severe levels of antisocial behavior. In extreme cases, antisocial children are easily identified by virtue of scoring highly on all dimensions, that is, frequent, severe, chronic, repetitive, and diverse antisocial behaviors. Characteristics of the behaviors are pivotal but not sufficient by themselves to account for clinical referral.

Referral for Treatment

Children do not refer themselves for treatment for antisocial behavior. Rather, adults—typically parents—identify the child as in need of treatment. Parents and other adults do not, of course, share a standard set of definitions, criteria, or thresholds for deciding when this point has been reached. Referral for clinical help depends on a number of factors such as judgments about the seriousness of the behaviors, judgments about the child or adolescent's functioning, pressures from others to intervene (e.g., the schools), the availability of other resources (e.g., assistance from relatives in caring for the child), and the parents' actual or perceived inability to manage the child.

The range of influences that dictate who is referred to treatment is not fully understood. Research has suggested that depression and anxiety of the mother is related to her perceptions of her child's behavior. Mothers higher in these dimensions perceive their children's behavior more negatively and hence are more likely to refer their children to treatment (Forehand, Wells, McMahon, Griest, & Rogers, 1982; Griest, Wells, & Forehand, 1979). Parental dysfunction (e.g., depression), family stressors (e.g., unemployment, marital discord), competing demands (e.g., rearing of other children, care of relatives), and other factors all may enter into delineation of children as clinically impaired.

Conduct Disorder and Delinquency

Characteristics of antisocial behavior (e.g., frequency, intensity) that may lead to clinical attention may also lead to referral of the child to the courts. Consequently, it is important to clarify the relation between conduct disorder and delinquency. Delinquency refers to a legal designation and usually is based on official contact with the courts. There are, however, specific behaviors that can be referred to as delinquent. These include offenses that are criminal if committed by an adult (e.g., homicide, robbery) as well as a variety of behaviors that are illegal because of the age of the youths. These latter acts, referred to as *status offenses,* involve the use of alcohol, driving a car, staying out late, not attending school, and other behaviors that would not be crimes if the youths were adults.

Conduct disorder and delinquency overlap in different ways but they are not the same. As already noted, conduct disorder refers to clinically severe antisocial behavior in which the everyday functioning of the individual is impaired, as defined by parents, teachers, and others. Conduct-disordered youths may or may not engage in behaviors that are defined as delinquent or have any contact with the police and courts. Official contact with police is unlikely to take place or to be recorded for young children (Empey, 1982). Delinquent acts in early and middle childhood usually are dealt with informally rather than officially. On the other hand, conduct disorder may be identified and brought to attention early as the child's behavior comes into conflict on a daily basis with parent and teacher expectations. Thus, conduct-disordered youths are not necessarily defined or viewed as delinquent. It is also possible that delinquent youths, adjudicated by the courts, would not be considered as conduct disorder. The youths may have committed crimes (homicide, selling of narcotics, prostitution) on one or more occasions but not be regarded as impaired, emotionally disturbed, or functioning poorly *in the context* of their everyday life.

Although a distinction can be drawn, many of the behaviors of delinquents and conduct-disordered youths overlap and fall under the general rubric of antisocial behavior. Moreover much of what has been learned about antisocial behavior has been derived from the study of delinquent youths. Typically, studies have evaluated adjudicated and incarcerated youths to try to understand their unique characteristics. The difficulty is that only a small fraction of persons who commit delinquent acts are detected and few of these are ever adjudicated (Empey, 1982). Thus, the information derived from incarcerated youths may not fully represent those who have not been adjudicated or, of course, those who are referred clinically. In recent years, large-scale evaluations have been conducted among normal children and adolescents who are asked to report on their delinquent and antisocial behaviors (e.g., Elliott, Knowles, & Canter, 1981; Farrington, 1978; Johnston, Bachman, & O'Malley, 1982). Such studies have shown much higher prevalence rates of antisocial and delinquent behaviors than official records usually reveal and have also provided important information regarding antisocial youths and their families.

CHARACTERISTICS OF CONDUCT DISORDER

Antisocial behaviors that emerge over the course of normal development are likely to be isolated, short-lived, and relatively mild. When the behaviors are extreme, do not remit over the course of development, affect the child's daily functioning, and have important implications for others (parents, teachers, peers), children are often brought to clinical attention. The antisocial behaviors then, of course, are viewed as significant departures from normal behavior and the children are often identified through mental health agencies or the courts.

Symptoms and Syndrome

Any specific antisocial act that children may evince can be viewed as an individual *symptom* or target behavior. Yet, several different antisocial behaviors are likely to occur together and to form a *syndrome* or constellation of symptoms. Conduct disorder, as a syndrome includes several core features such as fighting, engaging in temper tantrums, theft, truancy, destroying property, defying or threatening others, and running away, among others (see Quay, 1979). Obviously, any individual child is not likely to show all of the symptoms. The notion that they are all part of a syndrome merely notes that they are likely to come in packages.

Correlates and Associated Features

The above list of symptoms defines conduct disorder as a syndrome. There are other characteristics that are correlates or associated features rather than as defining characteristics. Among alternative symptoms that have been found among antisocial children, those related to *hyperactivity* have been the most frequently identified. These symptoms include excesses of motor activity, restlessness, impulsiveness, inattentiveness, and overactivity in general. In fact, the cooccurrence of hyperactivity and conduct disorder has made their diagnostic delineation and assessment a topic of considerable research. Several other behaviors have been identified as problematic among antisocial youths such as boisterousness, showing off, and blaming others (Quay, 1979). Many of these appear to be relatively mild forms of obstreperous behavior in comparison to aggression, theft, vandalism, or other acts that cause damage to persons or property.

Children and adolescents with conduct-disordered behaviors are also likely to suffer from *academic deficiencies*, as reflected in achievement level, grades, and specific skill areas, especially reading (e.g., Ledingham & Schwartzman, 1984; Sturge, 1982). Such children are often seen by their teachers as uninterested in school, unenthusiastic toward academic pursuits, and careless in their work (Glueck & Glueck, 1950). As would be expected from the above characteristics, conduct-disordered children are more likely to be left behind in grades, to show lower achievement levels, and to end their schooling sooner than their peers matched in age, socioeconomic status, and other demographic variables (Bachman, Johnson, & O'Malley, 1978; Glueck & Glueck, 1968).

Poor interpersonal relations are likely to correlate with antisocial behavior. Children high in aggressiveness or other antisocial behaviors are rejected by their peers and show poor social skills (e.g., Behar & Stewart, 1982; Carlson, Lahey, & Neeper, 1984). Such youths have been found to be socially ineffective in their interactions with an array of adults (e.g., parents, teachers, community members). Specifically, antisocial youths are less likely to defer to adult authority, to show politeness, and to respond in ways that promote further positive interactions (Freedman, Rosenthal, Donahoe, Schlundt, & McFall, 1978; Gaffney & McFall, 1981).

The correlates of antisocial behavior not only involve overt behaviors but also a variety of *cognitive and attributional processes*. Antisocial youths have been found to be deficient in cognitive problem-solving skills that underlie social interaction (Dodge, 1985; Kendall & Braswell, 1985). For example, such youths are more likely than their peers to interpret gestures of others as hostile and are less able to identify solutions to interpersonal problem situations and to take the perspective of others.

The above symptoms, correlated behaviors, and areas of impairment refer to *concurrent* problems that are likely to be evident in the behavior of clinically impaired children. A number of characteristics continue to emerge over time, as discussed in subsequent chapters.

Sex and Age Variations

Conduct disorder in children and adolescents varies as a function of sex (Gilbert, 1957; Robins, 1966). The precise sex ratio is difficult to specify because of varying criteria and measures of conduct disorder among the available studies. Nevertheless, antisocial behavior appears to be at least three times more common among boys (Graham, 1979). The sex differences are not merely due to biases in the referral process for identifying boys more than girls as problematic. Assessment of antisocial behavior through self-report reveals that male juveniles report higher rates of these behaviors than do females (Empey, 1982; Hood & Sparks, 1970).

Sex differences also are apparent in the age of onset of dysfunction. Robins (1966) found that the median age of onset of dysfunction for children referred for antisocial behavior was in the 8- to 10-year age range. Most (57%) boys had an onset before age 10 (median = 7 years old). For girls, onset of antisocial behavior was concentrated in the 14- to 16-year age range (median = 13 years old). Characteristic symptom patterns were different as well. Theft was more frequent as a basis of referral among antisocial boys than among antisocial girls. For boys, aggression was also likely to be a presenting problem. For girls, antisocial behavior was much more likely to include sexual misbehavior.

General Comments

Conduct disorder represents a major clinical and social problem. The behaviors, particularly aggression, are relatively frequent and account for the major portion of clinical referrals. Antisocial behaviors wax and wane over the course of normal development. When the behaviors are frequent, intense, and chronic, they raise a special problem. Children with clinically severe antisocial behaviors are likely to continue these behaviors as adolescents and adults. Moreover, the problems do not end in adulthood but continue through the offspring, so the cycle is sustained (Huesmann et al., 1984). Given the types of behaviors that are involved and their stability, conduct disorder is obviously costly to society. This can be illustrated pointedly by looking at monetary costs computed for individual problem areas such as vandalism, firesetting, or any other number of specific acts.

The personal or nonmonetary costs are monumental as well. Each individual story represents a personal tragedy. Sympathy for the conduct-disordered child or adolescent is easily evoked by detailing the personal situations and influences from which many such youths emerge. The sympathy is often lost when turning to the victims of antisocial acts, who may have had fortuitous contact with antisocial youths and were beaten, robbed, burned, or victimized in some other way. The salience of conduct disorder is agumented even further by the absence of clearly effective treatments. Thus, the clinical and social problems of conduct disorder thrive; the solutions in terms of understanding the dysfunctions and identifying steps to ameliorate them have a long germination period that has only just begun.

OVERVIEW OF REMAINING CHAPTERS

In subsequent chapters, the characteristics of conduct disorder will be elaborated. In Chapter 2, we will consider the diagnosis and assessment of conduct disorder. Alternative approaches to diagnosis of clinical disorders in general, specific methods to delineate types of conduct disorder, and strategies to measure antisocial behavior are examined. In Chapter 3, causes and risk factors will be identified. A great deal is known about who is likely to show severe antisocial behaviors and the factors that predict who will continue these behaviors into adulthood. An examination of risk factors elaborates the picture of the families of antisocial youths and the interpersonal and social environments from which they often emerge.

In Chapters 4 and 5, treatment and prevention are evaluated. The range of interventions that has been applied to antisocial youths or those who are at risk for conduct disorder is vast. Among the many innovative programs, only a few have been carefully evaluated and show promise at this point. The different programs, current status of treatment research, and the obstacles and prospects for identifying effective interventions are presented in Chapters 4 and 5.

In Chapter 6, approaches to the conceptualization, diagnosis, and treatment of conduct disorder are evaluated. Current work raises questions about the limitations of approaches that dominate the field. In this, the final chapter, new models are suggested that are designed to accelerate the rate of progress in ameliorating conduct disorder in children and adolescents.

NOTE

1. The term "conduct disorder" here is used generically to delineate clinically severe levels of dysfunction. In the next chapter, "conduct disorder" also refers to a specific constellation of behaviors in psychiatric diagnosis. The generic and specific uses of these terms overlap greatly. The proper noun will be used when the specific diagnostic category is delineated.

2

DIAGNOSIS AND ASSESSMENT

Information about how antisocial behaviors come about, what can be done in the way of treatment, and the likely long-term course all depend upon identifying cases of conduct disorder. Cases can vary widely in severity and type of dysfunction. For scientific advances, it is essential to specify the criteria to delineate dysfunction and to identify various symptom patterns. These objectives entail interrelated lines of work on the diagnosis and assessment of conduct disorder.

ALTERNATIVE APPROACHES TO DIAGNOSIS

The delineation of antisocial behavior through an agreed upon diagnostic system can greatly advance knowledge about alternative types of dysfunction, their causes, treatment, and prognosis. There are many different approaches toward diagnosis of childhood disorders in general (Achenbach, 1985). Clinically derived and multivariate approaches are discussed here because they reflect major approaches to child and adult psychopathology. Specific approaches that focus exclusively on antisocial behavior are presented as well.

Clinically Derived Diagnosis

Clinically derived diagnosis relies upon clinical observation and abstractions from these observations to identify discrete constellations of behaviors or syndromes. The resulting diagnostic systems have been *categorical* or typological. Various disorders are regarded as present or absent. The task of diagnosis is to identify which symptoms are present, if any, and then to assign or rule out the presence of discrete disorders. Several different clinically derived systems have been developed such as those advanced by the World Health Organization (1978), the Group for the Advancement of Psychiatry (1966), and the American Psychiatric Association (APA, 1980).

As an illustration, in the United States contemporary diagnostic practices are based on the third edition of the *Diagnostic and Statistical Manual of Mental Disorders* (DSM-III; APA, 1980).[1] The major diagnostic category within DSM-III for coding antisocial behavior in children and adolescents is Conduct Disorder. The essential feature of Conduct Disorder is a "repetitive and persistent pattern of conduct in which either the basic rights of others or major age-appropriate societal norms or rules are violated" (APA, 1980, p. 45). In order for the diagnosis to be made, the problematic behaviors must have a duration of at least six months. The diagnosis depends on the presence of several symptoms. Table 2.1 illustrates the type of symptoms that are included.

The precise criteria that are required to invoke a diagnosis of Conduct Disorder are currently under evaluation (APA, 1985). In the last official revision of the criteria for the DSM in 1980, four subtypes of Conduct Disorder were delineated based on the type of antisocial behavior (aggressive or nonaggressive) and the presence or absence of social attachments (socialized or undersocialized). Because a child is classified on each dimension, there are four different subtypes of Conduct Disorder (e.g., aggressive socialized, aggressive undersocialized, and so on). Children who meet the *aggressive* type violate the rights of others by force or physical violence (e.g., fighting, mugging, theft involving confrontation of the victim). Children who meet the *nonaggressive* type are characterized by the absence of physical violence as evident in such acts as running away, truancy, persistent lying or stealing, and vandalism. *Undersocialized* types are characterized by a failure to establish affection, empathy, and relationships with others. *Socialized* types show evidence of attachment and relationships with others.

There has been reconsideration of this fourfold classification because evidence is mixed regarding whether the types are distinguishable and predict different long-term patterns. Also, there are problems in making the diagnoses of subtypes. A given symptom (e.g., stealing or firesetting) might be classified as a sign of aggressive

Table 2.1 Symptoms Included in the Diagnosis of Conduct Disorder[a]

A period of six months or more during which some number of the following behaviors are evident. Specifically, the child or adolescent

1. is frequently truant
2. often "borrows" things from others without their permission
3. cheats in games with others or in school work
4. runs away (at least twice) from home (but not in reaction to physical or sexual abuse)
5. frequently initiates physical fights
6. has used a weapon in more than one fight
7. has forced someone into sexual activity
8. has been physically cruel to animals
9. has been physically cruel to other people
10. has deliberately destroyed property of others
11. has deliberately engaged in firesetting
12. has had voluntary sexual intercourse unusually early for his or her subculture
13. regularly uses tobacco, liquor, or other nonprescribed drugs and began their use unusually early
14. often lies in situations other than to avoid physical or sexual abuse
15. has broken into someone else's house, building, or car
16. has stolen outside of the home without confronting a victim on more than one occasion
17. has stolen outside of the home with confrontation of a victim

a. The symptom list here is based on the recent draft revisions of the *Diagnostic and Statistical Manual of Mental Disorders* (APA, 1985). At this point, the number of symptoms required to meet criteria for the diagnosis is scheduled to be derived from field tests of the criteria. In the current official version (DSM-III, APA, 1980), a diagnosis of conduct disorder could be made with the presence of a consistent pattern of one symptom (e.g., repeated physical violence against others).

or nonaggressive subtypes depending on circumstances not a part of the child's behavior or plans (e.g., whether a victim whose presence may have been unanticipated at the site of the theft, or whether the match play accidentally came out of control and burned or killed others). In current practices, most Conduct Disorder cases meet criteria for the Undersocialized Aggressive subtype. This does not mean that all of the youth's symptoms reflect aggressive behavior. Rather, aggression is typically a prominent symptom. The diagnosis of an aggressive subtype is usually based on whether any aggressive behavior is evident, even though other nonaggressive behaviors (e.g., truancy, lying) may be present as well.

Characteristics of conduct disorder may be evident in other diagnostic categories within DSM-III. Table 2.2 lists a number of diagnoses in which antisocial behaviors may also be evident. For each

Table 2.2 Other DSM-III Diagnostic Categories than Conduct Disorder that Include Antisocial Behaviors

Disorder or Condition and Key Characteristics
Oppositional Disorder
A pattern of disobedient, negativistic, and provocative opposition to authority figures as evident in such behaviors as violations of minor rules, temper tantrums, argumentativeness, or stubbornness. However, there are no major violations of the basic rights of others or societal norms or rules. The onset is between the ages of 3 to 18 years of age.
Adjustment Disorder with Disturbance of Conduct
A maladaptive reaction to an identifiable stressor that occurs within three months of the onset of that stressor (e.g., divorce, loss of a relative). The reaction includes impairment in daily functioning and symptoms that appear to be a direct reaction to that stressor. This diagnosis is reserved for the situation in which the symptoms include those of conduct disorder such as fighting, vandalism, and truancy.
Antisocial Personality Disorder
Characteristic antisocial behavior that is current and part of long-term functioning in which there is significant impairment in social or occupational areas or subjective distress. The diagnosis includes a pattern of continuous antisocial behavior. For this diagnosis, the individual must be at least 18 years old but the onset of the disorder was before age 15 and continuous over time.
Conditions Not Due to a Mental Disorder
Isolated antisocial acts rather than a pattern of antisocial behavior that suggests a longer-term mental disorder. Conflict between parent and child that does not appear to reflect a pattern of antisocial behavior or a mental disorder.

of these diagnoses, a critical feature such as age of onset or severity and duration of the behavior differs from that of Conduct Disorder. Oppositional Disorder is especially worth highlighting because the typical behaviors included in this diagnosis are likely to be evident in Conduct Disorder. However, children with a diagnosis of Oppositional Disorder do not show the major rule violations and serious antisocial acts of Conduct Disorder.

Multivariate Approaches

Multivariate approaches to diagnosis are fundamentally dimensional rather than categorical. Thus, the approaches do not lead to the statement that a person has a particular disorder. Rather, one can describe the degree to which one or many characteristics are evident.

Multivariate approaches depend upon determining the correlations among several specific characteristics (symptoms, problems) and then summarizing them through quantitative techniques (see Blashfield, 1984). Typically, the process begins by having parents, teachers, or others complete a measure that includes a large number of items about the child's behavior. Data obtained from a large number of children are subjected to *factor analysis* to identify symptoms (items) that go together (correlate). Rating scales yield multiple factors. An individual child has a score on each of the different factors or dimensions.

The information obtained from factor analysis can be used as the basis for constructing diagnostic categories or typologies. *Cluster analysis* is a set of procedures that can be used to move from scores on the factors to a typology. Through cluster analysis one can identify persons with similar patterns of scores across the different factors. The clusters serve as empirically derived diagnostic entities analogous to disorders derived from clinical methods.

Efforts to identify syndromes empirically have utilized a wide array of measures, raters, clinical samples, and methods of data analyses. Nevertheless, several similarities in the types of syndromes have emerged (see Achenbach, 1985; Quay, 1979). In factor analytic studies, conduct disorder has consistently emerged across age and gender groupings. The most common characteristics (or item content) associated with this factor are fighting, disobedience, temper tantrums, destructiveness, impertinence, and uncooperativeness (Quay, 1986). Cluster analyses to identify a typology of childhood disorders have been less frequently used. Even so, some consistencies have emerged here as well. Several studies using cluster analyses with normal, inpatient, and outpatient samples of children (ages 4 to 17) have identified clusters reflecting aggression and/or delinquent types of behaviors (e.g., Edelbrock & Achenbach, 1980; Lessing, Williams, & Gil, 1982).

Other empirical efforts have attempted to identify subtypes among children with antisocial behavior. For example, Quay (1964) evaluated case records of male delinquents (mean age 16.6) whose historical information was systematically rated by parole officers. The resulting factor analyses yielded four syndromes (with salient characteristics noted here in parentheses): (1) Socialized-Delinquent (delinquent behavior), (2) Unsocialized-Psychopathic (assaultive and defiant), (3) Overinhibited (neurotic, anxious, timid), and (4) Inadequacy-Immaturity (incompetent, unable to cope, sensitive).

Other multivariate analyses have yielded a larger number of subtypes. For example, one well-known system is referred to as the *I-Level Classification System* and has been developed with adjudicated delinquents.[2] The system was developed initially by obtaining extensive information (e.g., interview information, background data, behavioral ratings, sociometric ratings, and a variety of psychological tests) on institutionalized delinquents, ages 8 to 14 (Jesness, 1971). Through cluster analyses, based on ratings of several characteristics, nine subtypes of delinquents have been delineated (Jesness & Wedge, 1984): (1) Undersocialized Active, (2) Undersocialized Passive, (3) Conformist, (4) Group Oriented, (5) Pragmatist, (6) Autonomy Oriented, (7) Introspective, (8) Inhibited, and (9) Adaptive. The labels refer to the salient personality characteristics evident with each type. Evidence has suggested that these subtypes differ in various background characteristics, attitudes and aptitudes, and long-term prognoses for continued criminal behavior (Jesness & Wedge, 1984). Although the number of types identified vary considerably from those noted by Quay (1964), some commonalities can be identified. In both analyses the syndromes emerged on the basis of the type of behavior that is evident (e.g., aggressive, nonaggressive) and whether there are internalizing characteristics of the child (e.g., anxiety, inhibition, introspection).

Other multivariate analyses have been completed to develop broad diagnostic systems or to classify types of antisocial behavior (see Quay, 1979). From the research, it is clear that there is no single set or "real" number of subtypes that can be identified through multivariate approaches. Each set of results is qualified by and depends upon the sample, measures, and methods of data analysis. Yet, an important feature to look for is the consistency across studies where these dimensions vary. And, there have been consistencies such as the distinction of aggressive and delinquent types.

Other Diagnostic Approaches

Clinically derived and multivariate approaches used are designed to apply widely across a wide range of disorders rather than exclusively to antisocial behavior. Alternative approaches that focus exclusively on antisocial behavior have been proposed as well.

Salient Symptom Approach. One approach has been to identify salient symptoms and to determine if family characteristics, associated features, response to treatment, and prognosis vary among individuals with these symptoms. The unique feature of the approach is to identify individual symptoms that may yield reliable and clinically meaningful ways of segregating types of antisocial behavior. The approach is illustrated in the work of Patterson (1982) who has distinguished antisocial children whose primary symptom is aggression *(aggressors)* from those whose primary symptom is stealing *(stealers)*. Aggressors have a history of fighting and engaging in assaultive behavior; stealers have a history of repeated theft and contact with the courts. Although these characteristics often go together, subpopulations of "pure" aggressors or stealers can be readily identified.

Several studies have suggested the utility of distinguishing aggressors and stealers. For example, aggressive children have been found to engage in significantly more aversive and coercive behaviors in their interactions in the home and are less compliant with parents' requests than are children who steal (Patterson, 1982; Reid & Hendricks, 1973). Also, parents of stealers show greater emotional distance in relation to their children (e.g., lack of responding, less disapproval, fewer commands) than do parents of aggressors (Patterson, 1982).

Additional evidence suggests that families of aggressors and stealers respond differently to treatment. Parent management training has been effective in altering the coercive child-parent interactions that sustain deviant behavior among aggressors. However, coercive child-parent interactions apparently are not a central characteristic of family life among stealers. Although parents of stealers can be trained to apply parent management techniques, they are less likely to continue to apply them over time than are parents of aggressors. Other studies have shown that the prognosis of antisocial children may vary as a function of whether they have been identified as aggressors or stealers. For example, subsequent contact with the courts several years later is significantly more likely for children previously identified as stealers than aggressors (Moore, Chamberlain, & Mukai, 1979).

Interestingly, the salient symptom approach has not neglected the fact that many children are likely to be both aggressors and stealers. Indeed, the combination of salient symptoms may be significant in its own right. "Mixed" symptom children show characteristics of both types and are especially at risk for child abuse (Patterson, 1982).

Thus, the approach provides preliminary evidence regarding different salient symptom patterns.

Overt-Covert Types of Antisocial Behavior. This approach is related to the identification of salient symptoms but suggests a broader dimension that can be used to delineate subtypes. Antisocial behavior, according to this view, can be examined in relation to a bipolar dimension of overt and covert behavior (Loeber, 1985). *Overt behaviors* consist of those antisocial acts that are confrontive such as fighting, arguing, and temper tantrums. *Covert behaviors,* on the other hand, consist of concealed acts such as stealing, truancy, lying, and firesetting.

Loeber and Schmaling (1985a) analyzed a large number of studies that evaluated antisocial behavior of school-age children. Statistical analyses of the grouping of antisocial behaviors across studies supported the dimension of overt and covert behavior. Figure 2.1 shows the behaviors that are associated with each point on the dimension. The data indicated that overt behaviors tend to cluster together. This means that the presence of one overt behavior was likely to be associated with other overt behaviors. Similarly, the presence of a particular covert behavior is likely to be associated with other covert behaviors. As evident in the figure, some behaviors such as disobedience and sassiness tend to be present with both types of antisocial behavior.

Given the complexity and diversity of antisocial behaviors, one would expect that some children are likely to perform both overt and covert behaviors (i.e., reflect a mixed set of behaviors). Evidence suggests that mixed types of children are distinguished from purer types by more severe family dysfunction and poorer long-term prognoses, as reflected in subsequent contact with police and careers of antisocial behavior (Loeber & Schmaling, 1985b; McCord, 1980). Thus, children whose antisocial behavior are diverse or mixed (overt and covert) may be at high risk for long-term dysfunction (Robins, 1978).

A significant feature of both the salient symptom and overt-covert dimensional approach is that each can examine both pure and mixed types. Children may show either aggression (overt behaviors) or stealing (covert behaviors) or the combination of both. The typology then is really threefold by looking at separate ends of the dimension of overt and covert as well as those with mixed symptomatology.

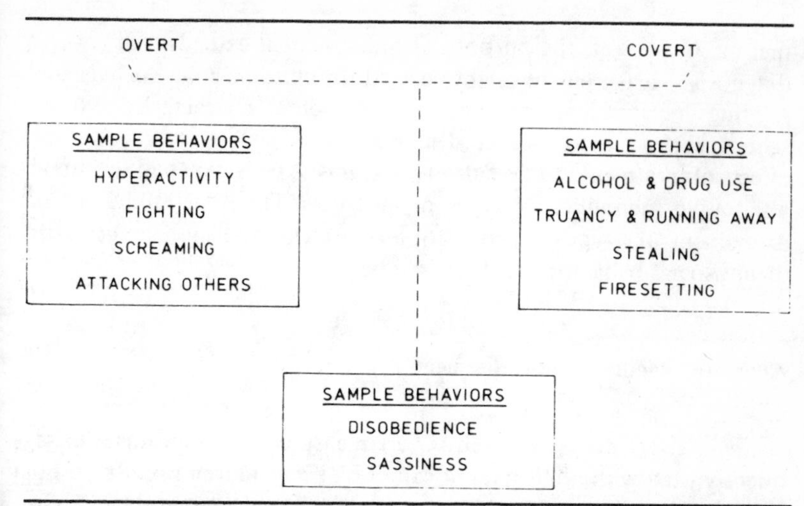

Figure 2.1 Overt-covert behavior as a dimension for delineating subtypes of antisocial behavior. Adapted from Loeber & Schmaling, 1985a.

General Comments

There are commonalities among clinically derived, multivariate, and other approaches. Obviously, each approach recognizes a constellation of antisocial behaviors among children and adolescents. Also, there are some consistencies in the subtyping of antisocial behavior. Although debate remains regarding fine delineations of antisocial behavior, each approach has suggested the importance of distinguishing an aggressive type (e.g., fighting) from a delinquent type (e.g., criminal behavior, running away, lying). The characteristics, prognoses, and developmental sequence of different types of antisocial behavior may be important. However, at present, the distinctions between subtypes of antisocial behavior and the effective approach for thwarting their development are not established.

ASSESSMENT OF ANTISOCIAL BEHAVIOR

Diagnosis refers to the different ways of classifying and delineating disorders. Alternative diagnostic methods rely upon some form of measurement. Yet, the purpose of measurement extends well beyond diagnosis. Measurement might be used for multiple goals such as correlating specific symptom patterns with other characteristics (e.g., school performance, parent discipline practices) or evaluating the effects of treatment or prevention programs. Assessment can rely upon alternative modalities or types of measures. Different modalities of assessment, the type of information they yield, and specific measures of antisocial behavior are discussed below.

Alternative Modalities of Assessment

Self-Report Measures. Self-report measures of symptoms are frequently used with adult patient samples. Yet, children usually do not identify themselves as having a problem or in need of treatment. Thus, one does not necessarily expect to see self-reported dysfunction with children or adolescents as one does with adults. Also, the ability of children to report on their dysfunction is less clear than for adolescents or adults. For these reasons, self-report is less heavily emphasized in the assessment of childhood disorders than it is for adult disorders.

Adolescents are more likely than children to be administered self-report measures. They more readily understand what is being asked and can complete paper-and-pencil measures with little or no assistance. Another reason that adolescents are more likely to receive self-report measures pertains to the availability of assessment tools. Measures developed for adults often are used in unmodified form with adolescents.

Although self-report is not usually used as the primary measure to evaluate childhood dysfunction, it can yield important information. Children can report on their symptoms and identify specific problem areas not always evident to their parents (Herjanic & Reich, 1982). Self-report may be especially valuable for measuring antisocial behaviors, particularly those behaviors that are likely to be concealed from parents. Information regarding such covert behaviors as vandalism, theft, or drug abuse are more readily reported by children and adolescents than by others or by institutional records (Elliott & Ageton, 1980; Williams & Gold, 1972). The validity of self-reported antisocial behaviors has been attested to in studies showing that they predict subsequent arrest and convictions as well as educational, employment, and marital adjustment (e.g., Bachman et al., 1978; Farrington, 1984).

Reports of Significant Others. Certainly reports of significant others (parents, teachers, therapists) are the most widely used measures of childhood disorders. Parents are the most frequently relied upon source of information given their obviously unique position in commenting on child functioning and changes over time. Moreover, studies have repeatedly shown that parent evaluations of children correlate with clinical judgments of child dysfunction.

As an assessment modality, measures completed by significant others have major advantages. Many rating scales are available that can be completed relatively quickly and can cover a wide range of symptom areas. There may be a partial bias in the types of antisocial behaviors that rating scales can assess. Behaviors such as teasing, fighting, yelling, arguing, and other overt acts are likely to be easily detected by parents and teachers. More covert acts such as stealing, substance abuse, and gang behavior, may be more difficult to assess. By their very nature, these latter behaviors may be hidden from the purview of the adult.

Peer Evaluations. Ratings by peers are worth distinguishing even though peers no doubt qualify as significant others. Also peer measures typically reflect an assessment methodology that departs from the rating scales used for parent and teacher assessments. Peer-based measures usually consist of different ways of soliciting peer nominations of persons who evince particular characteristics (e.g., aggressiveness). The consensus of the peer group is likely to reflect consistencies in performance and stable characteristics. Indeed, elementary school peer evaluations of aggressive behavior correlate with antisocial behavior years later (Huesmann et al., 1984).

Peer measures usually consist of sociometric ratings to identify such characteristics as popularity, likability, acceptance, rejection, and social competence. Such characteristics are quite relevant given the difficulties in each of these areas that antisocial children usually evince. Peer evaluations of social dimensions are correlated with independent evaluations of adjustment. Moreover, peer ratings occasionally are more sensitive as predictors of adjustment than are teacher and clinician ratings (e.g., Cowen, Pederson, Babigan, Izzo, & Trost, 1973; Rolf, 1972).

Direct Observation. The youth's specific behaviors at home, at school, or in the community can be observed directly. The key ingredients of direct observations are: defining behavior carefully, identifying the situations in which behavior will be observed, sending observers to record the behaviors, and ensuring that behavior is observed accurately and reliably. The requirements for direct observation vary as a function of the complexity of the assessment procedures. In clinical research, multiple behaviors are often observed in brief time intervals while the child interacts with his family at home (e.g., Patterson, 1982). In such cases, highly trained observers are needed to observe behavior. At the other extreme, one or two behaviors (e.g., episodes of stealing or fighting, school attendance) can be assessed at home or at school (see Kazdin, 1984). With relatively simple observational codes, parents and teachers can be used in place of trained observers.

An advantage of direct observations is they provide samples of the actual frequency or occurrences of particular antisocial or prosocial behaviors. Thus, the modality is distinguished from self-reports and reports of others that can be more influenced by judgments and impressions. Direct observations have their own liabilities. Many behaviors, especially covert acts (theft, drug use, sexual promiscuity), are not readily observed directly. Also, even when behaviors can be observed, the act of observation can influence their performance. Nevertheless, observation contributes unique information by sampling behavior directly.

Institutional and Societal Records. Evaluation of antisocial youths frequently relies on institutional records such as contact with the police, arrest records, attendance, grades, graduation, school suspensions and expulsions, and others. Institutional records are exceedingly important because they represent socially significant measures of the impact of the problem. Alternative governmental agencies at the state and national level monitor such events as the number of juvenile arrests or juvenile court cases. Such information can plot important social trends and facilitate decision making about allocation of resources and services for a particular problem.

There are many problems with institutional and societal records as a measure of antisocial behavior. Most antisocial and delinquent acts are not observed or recorded. In fact, research has suggested that 9 out of 10 illegal acts are not detected or not acted on officially (Empey, 1982). This conclusion has been supported by studies that ask children and adolescents to report on their delinquent and antisocial behaviors (Elliott & Ageton, 1980; Williams & Gold, 1972). Official records can greatly underestimate the incidence of antisocial behaviors because of the slippage between the occurrence of antisocial behavior and the ultimate recording of the act on some archival record. For example, arrest and conviction rates are obviously important but not particularly sensitive measures of delinquent behavior. Most crimes are not detected; those that are infrequently lead to arrest; those that do lead to arrest are not always referred to the court; those that are referred do not necessarily lead to conviction (Empey, 1982).

Notwithstanding the above limitations, institutional records are critical measures for the evaluation of antisocial behavior. Antisocial behavior by its very nature leaves its mark on society (e.g., vandalism, firesetting, crime statistics). Institutional records have often been used to measure the behavior of juveniles and to evaluate interventions designed to reduce antisocial behavior (e.g., Kirigin, Braukmann, Atwater, & Wolf, 1982; Offord et al., 1985).

General Comments. Each of the above modalities has its own strengths, methodological weaknesses, and sources of bias. For example, parent evaluations of deviant child behavior provide an obviously important and unique perspective given that parents usually are in an excellent position to comment on the child's functioning. Yet, parent evaluations are influenced by parent psychopathology and often fail to detect problems identified through child report or direct observation. Similarly, direct observation reflects performance of a particular behavior free from the global judgments and recollections of parents and teachers. Yet, the behaviors of interest may be too low in frequency or be performed when observers are not present. Hence, direct observation may miss many behaviors of interest. The concerns about any specific assessment modality could be multiplied (see Kazdin, 1980).

A particular modality may be especially relevant given the specific purposes of assessment. In most instances, multiple modalities should be included in an assessment battery. The reason is that the informa-

Table 2.3 Selected Measures of Antisocial Behaviors for Children and Adolescents

Measure	*Response Format*	*Age Range*	*Special Features*
Self-Report			
Children's Action Tendency Scale (Deluty, 1979)	30 items in forced-choice format, child selects what he would do in interpersonal situations.	6-15 years	Scores for response dimensions: aggressiveness, assertiveness, and submissiveness
Adolescent Antisocial Self-Report Behavior Checklist (Kulik, Stein, & Sarbin, 1968)	52 items, each of which is rated by the child on a 5-point scale (from never to very often).	Adolescence	The measure samples a broad range of behaviors from mild misbehavior to serious antisocial acts. The items load on 4 factors: delinquency, drug usage, parental defiance, and assaultiveness.
Interview for Antisocial Behavior (Kazdin & Esveldt-Dawson, in press; Kazdin, French, & Unis, 1983b)	Semistructured interview, 30 items pertaining to aggression and other antisocial acts. Each item rated on a 5-point scale for severity and a 3-point scale for duration.	6-13 years	Yields scores for severity, duration, and total (severity + duration) antisocial behavior. Separate factors assess overt and covert behaviors.
Children's Hostility Inventory (Kazdin, Rodgers, Colbus, & Siegel, in press)	38 true/false statements assessing different facets of aggression.	6-13 years	Derived from Buss-Durke Hostility Guilt Inventory. A priori subscales cover assaultiveness, indirect aggression, irritability, negativism, resentment, suspicion, verbal aggression, and guilt. Separate aggression and hostility scores are also available.

Self-Report Delinquency Scale (Elliott & Ageton, 1980)	47 items that measure frequency with which individual has performed offenses included in the Uniform Crime Reports. Responses provide frequency with which behavior was performed over the last year.	11-21 years	Developed as part of the National Youth Survey, an extensive longitudinal study of delinquent behavior, alcohol and drug use, and related problems in American youths.
Minnesota Multiphasic Personality Inventory Scales (Lefkowitz, Eron, Walder, & Huesmann, 1977)	True/false items derived from Scales F (test-taking attitude), 4 (psychopathic deviate) and 9 (hypomania) are summed to yield an aggression/delinquency score.	Adolescence	Part of a more general measure that assesses multiple areas of psychopathology.
Reports of Others			
Eyberg Child Behavior Inventory (Eyberg & Robinson, 1983)	36 items rated on 1 to 7 point scale for frequency and whether the behavior is a problem.	2-16 years	Designed to measure a wide range of conduct problems in the home.
Peer Nomination of Aggression (Lefkowitz, et al., 1977)	Items that ask children to nominate others who show the characteristics (e.g., "Who starts a fight over nothing"?).	3rd through 12th grade	Items reflect the child's reputation among peers regarding overall aggression. Different versions of peer nominations have been used.
Direct Observations			
Adolescent Antisocial Behavior Checklist[b] (Curtiss et al., 1983)	57 items to measure antisocial behavior during hospitalization. Behaviors are rated as having occurred or not based on staff observations.	Adolescence	The items can be scored using different sets of subscales; one set focuses on the form of the problem (e.g., physical vs. verbal harm); another set focuses on the objects of aggression (e.g., toward self, others, property). Different versions are available and differ in scoring.

Table 2.3 Continued

Measure	*Response Format*	*Age Range*	*Special Features*
Family Interaction Coding System (Reid, 1978)	Direct observational system to measure occurrence or nonoccurrence of 29 specific parent-child behaviors in the home. Each behavior is scored within small intervals for an hour each day for a period of several days.	3-12 years	Individual behaviors are observed but usually summarized with a total aversive behavior score. The general procedure can be adopted by using some or all of the behaviors of the FICS.
Parent Daily Report[b] (Patterson, Chamberlain, & Reid, 1982)	Parents identify symptoms of antisocial behavior. After symptoms are identified, the parent is called daily for several days. Each day the parent is asked if each behavior has or has not occurred in the previous 24-hour period.	3-11 years	Measure does not reflect a standardized set of items but rather refers more to an assessment approach for collecting data on behaviors at home.

a. This measure has separate versions: (1) a self-report measure for children, and (2) a parent-report measure to evaluate children's behavior.
b. This measure falls between rating by others and direct observation. Informants are asked to evaluate behavior but referents are highly specific acts within a particular time period.

tional yield and the conclusions that are drawn about the severity or type of dysfunction, the relation of the symptoms to other measures, and changes over time will vary for the different measures.

Alternative Measures

Measures of Antisocial Behavior. Relatively few measures have been developed specifically to assess antisocial behavior. Several currently available measures and their salient characteristics are enumerated in Table 2.3. A few measures are highlighted here to focus on characteristics not evident in the table.

Among the self-report measures, no single measure is in widespread use. The *Adolescent Antisocial Self-Report Behavior Checklist* (Kulik, Stein, & Sarbin, 1968) is noteworthy. The measure includes a broad range of behaviors from relatively minor acts to serious antisocial and delinquent acts. For example, sample items include skipping school, carrying a weapon, abusing alcohol or drugs, taking part in a robbery, hitting a teacher, and resisting arrest. Clearly, the behaviors reflect more than bothersome acts at home or the usual mischief that children are wont to do.

By way of contrast, consider the *Eyberg Child Behavior Inventory,* which is one of the more well-investigated measures of conduct problems for children ages 2 through 12 (Eyberg & Robinson, 1983; Robinson, Eyberg, & Ross, 1980). In this latter measure, completed by significant others, the focus is on problems the parents report at home for their conduct-problem children. Sample items include: verbally fighting with friends one's own age, refusing to do chores when asked, destroying objects, yelling or screaming. Most of the items reflect refusal and other oppositional behaviors that are annoying to parents rather than serious antisocial acts.

As an illustration of direct observational methods, the *Family Interaction Coding System* (FICS) warrants special mention (Patterson, 1982). The FICS has been used to record behaviors of antisocial children as they interact with their parents and siblings at home (Patterson, Reid, Jones, & Conger, 1975; Reid, 1978). More specifically, the measure is designed to assess aggressive behaviors and the antecedent and consequences (family interactions) with which they are associated. Among direct observation systems, the FICS is relatively elaborate. Twenty-nine different behaviors are coded by observers as present or absent in each of several brief time intervals (e.g., 30 seconds) over a period of approximately one hour. Prosocial and deviant child behaviors (e.g., complying with requests, attacking someone, yelling) and parent behaviors (e.g., providing approval, playing with the child, humiliating the child) are included.

The FICS has several important requirements. First, observers must be carefully trained and closely monitored to ensure that the codes are scored reliably. Second, the situations in which observers complete their assessment need to be partially controlled to limit the variability in the setting. For example, when the FICS is used in the home, families are instructed to remain in a small number of rooms during the period in which observations are obtained and not to watch television or to make outgoing phone calls, all of which help observers score child-parent interactions. The FICS and other, less complex, direct observational codes have been used frequently to assess antisocial behaviors at home and at school (Kazdin, 1984).

Overall, relatively few measures developed for antisocial behavior among children and adolescents have been in widespread use. Measures have been devised and utilized for a specific purpose as part of an ongoing research program. With few exceptions, little validational work has been conducted nor have normative data been provided to indicate the level of antisocial behavior for the measure over the course of normal development.

General Measures of Psychopathology. Most studies of antisocial behavior rely on measures that assess diverse areas of psychopathology and functioning. The reasons are manifold. To begin with, such measures provide information about the domain of interest and many other areas as well. This feature is important because children who suffer antisocial behavior may also show dysfunction in other areas (e.g., hyperactivity, anxiety). In addition, general measures of psychopathology offer a number of parent and teacher rating scales that have been well researched and validated.

Different types of measures are available that assess a broad range of symptoms and behaviors. *Diagnostic interviews* are used increasingly with children and adolescents. In such interviews, parent and child are interviewed separately to evaluate the presence and/or severity of the full range of symptoms. The goal is to permit the examiner to provide a diagnosis based on a specific diagnostic system (e.g., DSM-III, Research Diagnostic Criteria). Several diagnostic interviews have been developed for children and adolescents. Three examples include the *Schedule for Affective Disorders and Schizophrenia for School-Age Children* (K-SADS; Chambers et al., 1985); the *Diagnostic Interview for Children and Adolescents* (Herjanic & Reich, 1982); and the *Child Assessment Schedule* (Hodges, McKnew, Cytryn, Stern, & Kline, 1982).

Diagnostic interviews are valuable for delineating populations and identifying subtypes according to specific diagnostic criteria. However, the measures yield categorical information by classifying persons in one diagnostic group or another. In many cases, it is important to make finer distinctions along a dimension of severity of dysfunction or severity of specific symptoms. In such cases, dimensional measures such as various rating scales and checklists are likely to be more useful.

By far the most well-developed measures that assess multiple areas of child and adolescent dysfunction are *parent and teacher rating scales.* These scales present a large number of items that the parent or teacher rates in terms of presence or absence or severity of dysfunction. The *Child Behavior Checklist* (CBCL) is typical of such instruments where parents complete items to convey characteristics of their children. The measure includes 118 items that refer to behavior problems, each of which is rated on a 3-point scale (0 = not true, 2 = very or often true). Three sample items include: cruelty, bullying, or meanness to others; argues a lot; sets fires. The scale yields several different factors or constellations of symptoms including aggression, delinquency, hyperactivity, anxiety, depression, uncommunicativeness, schizophrenia, and others. The scale was analyzed separately for boys and girls in different age groups (4-5, 6-11, 12-16 years old). Consequently, with the CBCL, one can evaluate an individual child's standing on all the symptom scales or factors relative to same age and gender peers who have not been referred for treatment. Many other rating scales and checklists have been administered to parents. Prominent examples include the *Behavior Problem Checklist* (Quay, 1977), the *Parent Symptom Questionnaire* (Conners, 1970), the *Louisville Behavior Checklist* (Miller, Hampe, Barrett, & Noble, 1971), the *Institute for Juvenile Research Behavior Checklist* (Lessing, Williams, & Revelle, 1981), and the *Personality Inventory for Children* (Wirt, Lachar, Klinedinst, & Seat, 1977).

Teacher evaluations of child behavior also play a role in identification of childhood dysfunction. Teachers observe children for protracted amounts of time and across a wide range of situations (e.g., structured vs. unstructured classroom activities, academic, social and recreational settings). Moreover, the teacher can evaluate children in the context of their peers. A given child's departure from his or her peers provides a perspective that may not be available to parents. Teacher and parent rating instruments usually do not differ in structure or format. Indeed, many scales such as the *Behavior Problem Checklist* have been administered to parents, teachers, and other adults (e.g., clinic staff). For several measures, parallel forms exist for teachers and parents. Examples include the *CBCL-Teacher Report Form* (Achenbach & Edelbrock, 1983), the *Conners Teachers Questionnaire* (Conners, 1969), and the *School Behavior Checklist* (Miller, 1972) that are parallel to forms mentioned above for parents.

As an assessment modality, parent and teacher rating scales have been widely used. Their value derives from sampling a wide spectrum of symptom areas and from their ease of administration. Considerable data have been generated on their use and psychometric properties (reliability and validity). Also, normative data are available for many measures that permit comparison of clinic and nonclinic samples and variations in symptom areas as a function of age, gender, social class, and other subject or demographic variables.

CURRENT ISSUES AND LIMITATIONS

Delineation of Conduct Disorder

Major advances have been made in the diagnosis of conduct disorder and other disorders more generally. For example, in the third edition of the DSM, criteria for invoking diagnoses have been better specified than in previous editions. Nevertheless, there is still a lack of *operational criteria* that denote specific measurement strategies and cutoff scores on these measures that can be used to identify diagnostic groups (cf. Loney, 1983). Thus, exactly how to measure conduct disorder is not well worked out.

In contemporary work, the identification of conduct disorder has been inconsistent. For example, relatively high scores on specific parent rating scales (e.g., externalizing scale of the CBCL), clinical diagnoses obtained informally from an unstructured interview or a review of institutional records, referrals from teachers of children who are behavioral problems, and parental responses to advertisements to recruit children who are unmanageable all have been used to identify conduct-disordered children. It is very likely that some children selected with any of the above procedures would meet diagnostic criteria (e.g., DSM-III) for Conduct Disorder. Yet, current evidence suggests that many children who meet diagnostic criteria for Conduct Disorder may also meet criteria for Attention Deficit Disorder (ADD) with hyperactivity (see Prinz, Conner, & Wilson, 1981; Stewart, DeBlois, Meardon, & Cummings, 1980). The disorders can be distinguished and youths who meet criteria for one do not necessarily meet criteria for the other. However, making the distinction requires careful assessment.

In much of the work on antisocial behavior, assessment procedures do not permit careful delineation of the sample. Whether antisocial behaviors are present, severe, or primary as a presenting problem or whether the children are overactive and bothersome to teachers and/or parents are not easily discerned. The ambiguous and inconsistent identification of samples for clinical research makes it difficult to know the characteristics of a particular sample and to compare different samples across studies.

In general, it is important to develop further criteria that will be used to define conduct disorder and the manner in which these criteria will be assessed. To make further advances, there need not be agreement on the many complex questions such as the subtypes of conduct disorder and the organization of symptom patterns. Rather, these questions can be better served by attempts to utilize standardized measures and explicit criteria to select samples for further research.

Convergence of Different Measures

As a more general problem, diverse measures of child behavior (parent, teacher, self-report ratings, and direct observations) may show little or no correlation. For example, there is little or no agreement between parents and children when they each complete the identical measure to assess antisocial child behavior or other dysfunctions (Kazdin, Esveldt-Dawson, Unis, & Rancurello, 1983a, 1983c). Some evidence suggests that children tend to underestimate the presence and severity of their symptoms when parallel information is obtained from other sources (Kazdin, French, Unis, & Esveldt-Dawson, 1983c; Orvaschel, Puig-Antich, Chambers, Tabrizi, & Johnson, 1982). Many behaviors, particularly antisocial behaviors (e.g., firesetting, stealing, running away, breaking school rules, trying to kill someone), are not as likely to be perceived *as a problem* for children as they are for parents (see Herjanic & Reich, 1982). Yet, underreporting is not sufficient to explain the lack of correspondence among different sources of information.

Different assessment modalities imperfectly measure the behaviors of interest and are influenced by multiple factors. For example, noted already were the findings that parent report of deviant child behavior depends on the parent's own symptoms of psychopathology (especially depression and anxiety), marital discord, expectations of child behavior, parent self-esteem, and reported stress in the home (e.g., Griest & Wells, 1983; Mash & Johnston, 1983). In general, the lack of agreement among different sources of information regarding child symptoms seems to be a function of the source of information (e.g., mother, father, child); different perspectives (e.g., parents, teachers, mental health workers); and the types of behaviors (e.g., subjective versus overt signs) (Herjanic & Reich, 1982; Kazdin, French, & Unis, 1983b; Kenrick & Stringfield, 1980; Ledingham, Younger, Schwartzmann, & Bergeron, 1982).

At present there is no simple way to determine which measure reflects true performance. The lack of objective criteria against which to evaluate alternative measures makes it difficult to evaluate a given measurement technique. Some attempts have been made to validate different measures against direct observation of overt behavior. Discrepancies between parent or teacher reports and measures of overt behavior are common. However, direct observations raise their own problems. They do not always sample broadly across behaviors or situations, and the specific codes may not reflect the salience or significance of the symptom (e.g., for low frequency but highly significant behaviors such as firesetting or stealing). Although direct observations may provide concrete and clear criteria for scoring behavior, they also fail to provide a flawless criterion against which other measures can be validated (Kazdin, 1979).

What to Assess?

The discussion has focused on the assessment of antisocial behavior and various measures that might be used toward that end. Yet, conduct disorder in children and adolescents is associated with a wide range of other characteristics that may be of interest for assessment purposes. For example, among conduct problem youths, measures of cognitive processes, social skills, and academic functioning are obvious areas that come to mind. The child's behavior in each of these, and related areas, may be as important and as dysfunctional as the specific antisocial behaviors that may have served as the basis for referral. Similarly, because of the strong association of family variables with childhood antisocial behavior, measures of marital discord, parent psychopathology, and life events are relevant as well. Given the pervasiveness of child, parent, and family dysfunction in severe cases of antisocial behavior, it is difficult to delimit the relevant measures to a circumscribed set.

General Comments

There are many ambiguities in both diagnosis and assessment of conduct disorder. The overlap of diagnoses such as conduct disorder and hyperactivity and the lack of operational criteria are especially important to bear in mind when reference is made to conduct disorder. The multiple assessment methods and their different results in regard to the characteristics of a particular child also raise ambiguities. Information from different sources (child, parent, teacher) provides valid information that correlates with other criteria but the sources may show little correlation with each other. There is at present no objective measure of conduct disorder that is free of some source of bias, artifact or judgment. The use of several different measures is essential to overcome the limitations of any single modality or scale.

SUMMARY AND CONCLUSIONS

The present chapter reviewed alternative approaches to the diagnosis of antisocial behavior in children and adolescents. Clinically derived and multivariate approaches were highlighted. These approaches can diagnose a broad range of childhood disorders, in addition to antisocial behavior. Other approaches that focus exclusively on antisocial behavior include the identification of salient symptoms (e.g., aggression vs. stealing) and the dimension of overt-covert behaviors. Across all diagnostic approaches, basic issues remain to be resolved regarding how antisocial behavior should be delineated. There are some points of convergence among alternative approaches such as the distinction of aggressive versus delinquent types. However, these types are quite heterogeneous and not invariably distinct.

Ideally, it would be useful to have an agreed upon set of diagnostic and assessment criteria that were in widespread use. To date, there has been no consistent diagnostic system utilized for a sufficient period of time to develop a cohesive body of information. Progress is evident in both clinically derived and multivariate approaches. For example, the specification of descriptive criteria for invoking DSM-III diagnoses and the emergence of diagnostic interviews to assess symptoms are important advances. Also, increasingly sophisticated assessment tools and methods of data analysis for multivariate approaches represent important advances for describing and classifying antisocial behavior.

The assessment of antisocial behavior has relied upon a number of alternative types of measures including interviews, self-report, parent, teacher, and peer ratings, direct observations, and institutional records. The kinds of information such measures provide and the interpretive problems they raise were identified briefly. Diagnosis and assessment are fundamental to research that is designed to understand the nature of antisocial behavior, its causes, correlates and clinical course. Measures that apply to diverse disorders of childhood and adolescence have received a great deal of attention and are relatively well developed. In contrast, there remains a need to develop measures that focus exclusively on the broad range of antisocial behaviors. Such measures can elaborate the range of behaviors and perhaps identify subtypes of antisocial behavior that will have important implications for early detection, prevention, and treatment.

NOTES

1. There are several distinguishing features of this system including the focus on the descriptive features or the presenting symptoms rather than their presumed etiology and delineation of specific criteria that define a disorder. In addition, patient behavior is evaluated on five separate dimensions or axes that code psychiatric impairment and other relevant characteristics. The multiple axes include: Axis I: Clinical Psychiatric Syndromes and Other Conditions; Axis II: Personality Disorders and Specific Developmental Disorders; Axis III: Physical Disorders; Axis IV: Severity of Psychosocial Stressors; and Axis V: Highest Level of Adaptive Functioning the Past Year. For an elaboration of these axes and applications to children, other sources can be consulted (see Kazdin, 1983; Rapoport & Ismond, 1984).

2. The "I" refers to the integration level of the individual. The theory underlying the classification system focuses on the individual's cognitive and personality development. As children grow, the theory posits, higher levels of integration of their experiences, perceptions, and awareness are evident. The different subtypes of delinquency are considered to reflect different levels of this integration (see Jesness & Wedge, 1984).

3

CAUSES AND RISK FACTORS

Antisocial behavior emerges lawfully and as a function of multiple influences, two assumptions that have contributed to important progress in research conducted to date. The overriding questions that follow from these assumptions are: who is likely to become antisocial and what are the factors leading to antisocial behavior? Needless to say, a simple statement cannot be made regarding the specific factors that *cause* antisocial behavior. The very complexity of human behavior in general, the different levels of influence (e.g., biological, psychological, and sociological), and the heterogeneity of behaviors referred to as "antisocial" preclude simple answers. Nevertheless, a great deal can be said about the influences that place children at risk for antisocial behavior and the likely mechanisms through which many of these influences operate.

RISK FACTORS FOR THE ONSET OF CONDUCT DISORDER

The initial question is whether one can identify factors that place a child at risk for antisocial behavior. To be "at risk" refers to the increased likelihood, above base rates in the population, that persons will show the behavior of interest. The factors that predispose children and adolescents to antisocial behavior have been studied extensively in the context of clinical referrals and adjudicated delinquents (e.g., Glueck & Glueck, 1950; Loeber & Dishion, 1983; Robins, 1966; Rutter & Giller, 1983; Wadsworth, 1979; West, 1982). The list of factors that have been implicated is quite long. Major categories addressed below include child, parent and family, and school-related factors.

Child Factors

Child Temperament. Temperament appears to be related to the emergence of conduct disorder. Temperament refers to those prevailing aspects of personality that show some consistency across situations and time (Plomin, 1983). The basis for these characteristics are considered to be genetic or constitutional, a view attributed in part to the fact that differences can be identified among children very early in life.

Differences in temperament are often based on such characteristics as activity of the child, emotional responsiveness, quality of moods, and social adaptability (Thomas & Chess, 1977). For example, one dimension of temperament utilized to distinguish children is "easy-to-difficult" (Plomin, 1983). Easy children are characterized by positive mood, approach toward new stimuli, adaptability to change, and low-intensity reactions to new stimuli. Children who are difficult and who show opposite patterns on the above characteristics are likely to show behavioral problems concurrently and/or to develop these problems later, compared to children who are less difficult (e.g., Earls, 1981; Reitsma-Street, Offord, & Finch, 1985). Difficult children are also more likely to be referred for treatment for aggressive behavior and tantrums (Rutter, Birch, Thomas, & Chess, 1964).

The reasons why a specific temperament might place children at risk for antisocial behavior are not clear. Parent-child interaction patterns along with temperament may influence the emergence of antisocial behavior. For example, evidence suggests that mothers may emit more negative behaviors to children who are difficult, to be ineffective in their control of deviant child behavior, and to reinforce through submissive responses, their child's demanding and aversive behavior (Patterson, 1982; Webster-Stratton & Eyberg, 1982). Although finer-grained analyses of temperament are needed in relation to the emergence of antisocial behavior, current evidence suggests that a difficult temperament early in childhood increases a child's risk for subsequent antisocial behavior.

Neuropsychological Functioning. Neurological abnormalities (e.g., soft signs, EEG aberrations, seizure disorders) have been of interest because they occur more frequently in antisocial adults than in various control samples (see McCord, 1982). Yet, gross neurological abnormalities have been inconsistently correlated with antisocial behavior. With children and adolescents, antisocial behavior and neurological dysfunction have been associated in some studies (Lewis, Pincus, Shanok, & Glaser, 1982; Lewis, Shanok, Pincus, & Glaser, 1979) but not in others (Hsu, Wisner, Richey, & Goldstein, 1985; McManus, Brickman, Alessi, & Grapentine, 1985). Neurological abnormalities appear to be associated with childhood dysfunction more generally rather than conduct disorder or aggression in particular (Rutter, 1981). Overall, the findings on neurological signs are difficult to interpret. Also, because antisocial children are more likely to have head and face injuries, and more hospital visits, and to be victims of child abuse than nondelinquent children (Shanok & Lewis, 1981), early neurological signs, when evident, may well be the result of risk-taking behavior and adverse family conditions (e.g., abuse of the child).

Subclinical Levels of Antisocial Behavior. Several studies have found that subclinical levels of antisocial behavior predict later conduct disorder and delinquency. Teacher and peer measures of aggressiveness and unmanageability early or late in one's school years predict subsequent antisocial behavior (e.g., Glueck & Glueck, 1959; Mitchell & Rosa, 1981; West & Farrington, 1973). These behaviors can be called "subclinical levels" because they are not of the severity that lead to clinical referral. Although there is a clear continuity of problematic behavior, this does not mean that all or indeed even most youths with obstreperous behavior are identified later as antisocial. However, early child behavior is one of the more robust predictors of later conduct disorder. We will return to characteristics of the child's early antisocial behavior later, because specific characteristics of that behavior (e.g., age of onset, number of different types of antisocial behavior) are important predictors of continued antisocial behavior in adulthood.

Academic and Intellectual Performance. As noted earlier, academic deficiencies and lower levels of intellectual functioning are associated with conduct disorder. This relation has been demonstrated with diverse measures of intellectual and school performance such as verbal and nonverbal tests, grades, achievement tests and measures of antisocial behavior such as self-report, teacher report, and official records of delinquency (see Rutter & Giller, 1983; West, 1982). Of course, the association does not necessarily mean that academic dysfunction represents a risk factor. Reduced time at school (e.g., truancy, expulsion) and less attention from teachers might lead to poor academic achievement. However, evidence suggests that academic deficiencies and lower IQ predict subsequent antisocial behavior (Hirschi & Hindelang, 1977; Wadsworth, 1979; West, 1982).

Academic and intellectual functioning are known to be related to other variables such as socioeconomic class and family size. Even when these variables are controlled, educational and intellectual functioning serve as predictors of antisocial behavior (West & Farrington, 1973; West, 1982). Although academic dysfunction is a risk factor for subsequent conduct disorder, the relation is not merely unidirectional. Antisocial behavior predicts subsequent failure at school and level of educational attainment (Bachman et al., 1978; Ledingham & Schwartzmann, 1984).

Parental Factors

Psychopathology and Criminal Behavior. Psychopathology in the parents places the child at risk for psychological disturbance in general (Rutter et al., 1970). As might be expected, the risk for antisocial behavior in the child is more specifically related to the presence of such behaviors in either parent. Criminal behavior and alcoholism, particularly of the father, are two of the stronger and more consistently demonstrated parental factors that increase the child's risk for conduct disorder (Robins, 1966; Rutter & Giller, 1983; West, 1982).

Interestingly, selected antisocial and associated behaviors are highly related between parent and child. For example, Robins (1978) reported the relation between school truancy and dropping out of high school between parents and their children. If one (vs. neither) parent evinced either of these behaviors, the risk for the child showing the same behavior was greater. If both parents showed the behavior, the risk was greater still. This study shows that specific antisocial and maladaptive parental behaviors, through whatever mechanism, clearly increase the risk for these same behaviors in their offspring.

Most studies of parental dysfunction have focused on the parents of the antisocial child. Grandparents of antisocial children and adolescents, on both paternal and maternal sides, are more likely to show antisocial behavior (criminal behavior and alcoholism) compared to the grandparents of youths who are not antisocial (Glueck & Glueck, 1968). Longitudinal studies have shown that aggressive behavior is stable across generations within a family. More specific statements can be made. For example, a good predictor of how aggressive the child will be is the level of aggressiveness of the father when he was about the same age (Huesmann et al., 1984). In general, a previous history of antisocial or aggressive behavior in one's family places children at risk for these behaviors.

Parent-Child Interaction. Several features related to the interaction of parents with their children are risk factors for conduct disorder. Parent disciplinary practice and attitudes have been especially well studied. Parents of delinquent and conduct-disordered youths tend to be harsh in their attitudes and disciplinary practices with their children (e.g., Farrington, 1978; Glueck & Glueck, 1968; McCord, McCord, & Howard, 1961; Nye, 1958). Studies have also shown the degree of child aggression in nonclinic populations is positively correlated with severity of punishment in the home (e.g., Sears, Maccoby, & Levin, 1957). Indeed, conduct-disordered youths are more likely than normals and clinical referrals without antisocial behavior to be victims of child abuse and to be in homes where spouse abuse is evident (Behar & Stewart, 1982; Lewis et al., 1979; Lewis, Shanok, Grant, & Ritvo, 1983).

The increased risk for antisocial behavior apparently is not due simply to harsh punishment. Studies have shown that more lax, erratic, and inconsistent discipline practices within a given parent and between the parents are related to delinquency. For example, severity of punishment on the part of the father and lax discipline on the part of the mother has been implicated in delinquent behavior (Glueck & Glueck, 1950; McCord, McCord, & Zola, 1959). When parents are consistent in their discipline practices, even if they are punitive, children are less likely to be at risk for delinquency (McCord et al., 1959).

Apart from punishment practices, research suggests that the other ways of controlling child behavior are problematic among parents of antisocial youths. Direct observation of families in the home has revealed that parents of antisocial children are more likely to give commands to their children, to reward deviant behavior directly through attention and compliance, and to ignore or provide aversive consequences for prosocial behavior (see Patterson, 1982). Fine-grained analyses of parent-child interaction suggest that antisocial behavior, particularly aggression, is systematically albeit unwittingly trained in the homes of antisocial children.

Supervision of the child, as another aspect of parent-child contact, has been frequently implicated in conduct disorder (Glueck & Glueck, 1968; Goldstein, 1984; Robins, 1966). Parents of antisocial or delinquent children are less likely to monitor their children's whereabouts or to make arrangements for their care when they are temporarily away from the home. Other factors considered to reflect poor supervision and to constitute risk factors include the absence of rules in the home stating where the children can go and when they must return home, allowing children to roam the streets, and permitting them to engage in many independent and unsupervised activities (Wilson, 1980).

Features that reflect the quality of parent-child and family relationships also have been identified as risk factors. Parents of antisocial youths, compared with parents of normal youths, show less acceptance of their children, less warmth, affection, and emotional support, and report less attachment (Loeber & Dishion, 1984; McCord et al., 1959; West & Farrington, 1973). At the level of family relations, less supportive and more defensive communications among family members, less participation in activities as a family, and more clear dominance of one family member also distinguish families of antisocial youths (Alexander, 1973; Hanson, Henggeler, Haefele, & Rodick, 1984; West & Farrington, 1973).

Broken Homes and Marital Discord. Separation of one's parents during childhood (broken homes) has been found to be related to antisocial child behavior and delinquency (Glueck & Glueck, 1968; McCord et al., 1959; Nye, 1958). Yet, broken homes are related to psychiatric impairment across a variety of disorders in children and are not unique to conduct disorder (Rutter et al., 1970). Also, the separation of the parents may be due to several factors such as death, institutionalization or marital discord. Research has consistently demonstrated that unhappy marital relationships, interpersonal conflict, and aggression characterize the parental relations of delinquent and antisocial children (see Hetherington & Martin, 1979; Rutter & Giller, 1983). Whether or not the parents are separated, it is the extent of discord that is associated with the risk for antisocial behavior and childhood dysfunction (Hetherington, Cox, & Cox, 1979). Even so, discord or separation may only serve as risk factors when they occur early in the child's life, for instance, within the first 4 or 5 years (Wadsworth, 1979), and still do not serve as a strong predictor of conduct disorder.

Birth Order and Family Size. Birth order is related to the onset of antisocial behavior. Research has suggested that delinquency and antisocial behavior are greater among middle children in comparison to only, first born, or youngest children (e.g., Glueck & Glueck, 1968; McCord et al., 1959; Nye, 1958; Wadsworth, 1979). The effects are complex and, in the case of delinquency, may vary as a function of type of offense and duration of only-child status (e.g., before a sibling is born). However, in general, an extended period of time as the only or the youngest child before the sibling is born reduces risk for delinquency (Wadsworth, 1979).

Family size has frequently been shown to relate to delinquency with more children in the family associated with higher rates of delinquency (Glueck & Glueck, 1968; Nye, 1958; West, 1967). Family size obviously relates to findings of birth order of the children. Efforts to separate them have looked at birth spacing of offspring and family size. Children with older siblings are more likely to be delinquent, and the older the siblings (i.e., space in age between them), the greater the likelihood of delinquency (Wadsworth, 1979). Interestingly, the risk is associated with the number of brothers rather than sisters in the family (Offord, 1982). If one of the brothers is antisocial, the others are at increased risk for antisocial behavior (Robins, West, & Herjanic, 1975).

Social Class. There is a preponderance of conduct disorder and delinquency from lower socioeconomic classes (West, 1982). However, interpretation of this finding is complicated because of the association of social class with family size, overcrowding, poor child supervision, and other variables that have been identified as risk factors. When these separate factors are controlled, social class shows little or no relation to antisocial behavior (Robins, 1978; Wadsworth, 1979). Yet, in many instances, the impact of separate factors is not evaluated. Social class, as a summary label or conglomerate variable that includes a number of class-related factors, can be considered as a measure of risk.

School-Related Factors

Characteristics of the Setting. The school setting has been studied as contributing to risk of antisocial behavior. Schools can be characterized in many ways including their organization, locale, teacher-student ratio, and other characteristics that are often difficult to separate from each other and to distinguish from the selection factors of the students and families they serve. Selected characteristics are associated with antisocial behavior. For example, elementary or primary schools that are in poor physical condition or that have a low teacher-student ratio have higher rates of delinquency (Wadsworth, 1979).

Rutter and his colleagues (1979) examined 12 different secondary schools and their association with child behavior outcomes, including attendance, continuation in school, delinquency rates, and academic performance. Several characteristics of the schools influenced more favorable outcomes including an emphasis on academics, teacher time on lessons, teacher use of praise and appreciation for school work, emphasis on individual responsibility of the students, good working conditions for pupils (e.g., clean classroom, furniture in good repair), availability of the teacher to deal with children's problems, and consistent teacher expectancies, among others. The overall findings indicated reliable differences among schools on the outcome measures that could not be accounted for simply by differences in physical characteristics of the schools (size, available space) or recruitment of the different types of children and families. Moreover, data suggested that the combination of several factors (noted above) rather than any single variable contributed to more favorable child outcomes. In any case, characteristics of the school may contribute to antisocial behavior and serve as a risk factor.

General Comments

The list of risk factors is not complete. Within categories mentioned above, additional risk factors could be identified such as mental retardation of the parent, early marriage of the parents, lack of parent interest in the child's school performance, lack of participation of the family in religious or recreational activities, and many other parent and family factors (Glueck & Glueck, 1968; Wadsworth, 1979). Additional categories of factors might be conveyed as well, each with its own set of variables. For example, no mention was made of the influence in childhood of exposure to violent and aggressive television that has been shown to increase the risk for aggressive behavior over the course of adolescence and adulthood (Lefkowitz et al., 1977). The primary purpose was to identify major factors that relate to risk. Reviews of multiple studies suggest that parent, family and educational factors in addition to early signs of deviant behavior in the children themselves are the more robust predictors of conduct disorder and delinquency (see Loeber & Dishion, 1983; Rutter & Giller, 1983; West, 1982).

Even by restricting the discussion to major predictors, it appears that an almost endless array of factors place the child at risk. However, many of the factors discussed separately are interrelated and come in "packages." For example, family size, overcrowding, poor housing, poor parental supervision, parent criminality, and marital discord are likely to be related. Thus, the long list of risk factors reflects different ways of identifying related, or at least overlapping factors. Identification of the unique contribution of any specific factor requires a careful effort to partial out other factors with which it may be associated. This has not always been accomplished.

Apart from their cooccurrence, individual risk factors may interact with each other. For example, larger family size has been repeatedly shown to be a risk factor for conduct disorder and delinquency. However, the importance of family size as a predictor is moderated by (i.e., interacts with) income. If family income and living accommodations are adequate, family size is less likely to be a risk factor. Family size exerts a greater influence on risk in lower family income homes where overcrowding and other problems are likely to emerge (West, 1982). Apparently, families with adequate income can manage larger numbers of children and reduce the impact of any adverse influences associated with lower socioeconomic disadvantage.

The dependence of individual risk factors on other variables has also been evident in academic and educational performance. For example, intelligence test performance and reading and word comprehension predict subsequent delinquency, as noted earlier. Yet, intelligence of the child is related to socioeconomic status and family size. When these two factors are controlled, intelligence does not always remain as a predictor of delinquency (Wadsworth, 1979). As a general statement it is useful, especially for didactic purposes, to refer individually to the risk factors. However, the statements about the influence of any particular factor may need to be qualified by other variables with which it interacts. Considerably less is known about the multiple interactions that are possible among risk factors.

CONTINUATION OF CONDUCT DISORDER IN ADULTHOOD

The above discussion addresses factors that increase risk for onset of conduct disorder. Once children engage in serious antisocial behaviors, to what extent will these behaviors continue? The poor prognosis of conduct disorder is fairly well established. Longitudinal studies have consistently shown that delinquent or clinically referred antisocial behavior identified in childhood or adolescence predicts a continued course of social dysfunction, problematic behavior, and poor school adjustment (e.g., Bachman et al., 1978; Gersten, Langner, Eisenberg, Simcha-Fagan, & McCarthy, 1976; Glueck & Glueck, 1968; Jessor & Jessor, 1977; McCord et al., 1959).

One of the most dramatic illustrations of the long-term prognosis of clinically referred children was the classic study by Robins (1966) who evaluated their status 30 years later. The results demonstrated that antisocial child behavior predicted multiple problems in adulthood. Youths who had been referred for their antisocial behavior, compared to youths with other clinical problems or matched normal controls, as adults suffered dysfunction in psychiatric symptoms, criminal behavior, physical health, and social adjustment.

Table 3.1 Long-Term Prognosis of Youths Identified as Conduct Disorder: Overview of Major Characteristics Likely to Be Evident in Adulthood

Area of Functioning	*Characteristics in Adulthood*
1. Psychiatric Status	Greater psychiatric impairment including antisocial personality, alcohol and drug abuse, and isolated symptoms (e.g., anxiety, somatic complaints); also, greater history of psychiatric hospitalization
2. Criminal Behavior	Higher rates of driving while intoxicated, criminal behavior, arrest records, and conviction, and period of time spent in jail; greater seriousness of the criminal acts
3. Occupational Adjustment	Less likely to be employed; shorter history of employment, lower status jobs, more frequent change of jobs, lower wages, and depend more frequently on financial assistance (welfare). Served less frequently and performed less well in the armed services
4. Educational Attainment	Higher rates of dropping out of school, lower attainment among those who remain in school
5. Marital Status	Higher rates of divorce, remarriage, and separation
6. Social Participation	Less contact with relatives, friends, and neighbors; little participation in organizations such as church
7. Physical Health	Higher mortality rate; higher rate of hospitalization for physical (as well as psychiatric) problems

NOTE: These characteristics are based on comparisons of clinically referred children identified for antisocial behavior relative to control clinical referrals or normal controls or from comparisons of delinquent and nondelinquent youths (see Bachman et al., 1978; Glueck & Glueck, 1950; Huesmann et al., 1984; Robins, 1966, 1978; Wadsworth, 1979).

Several studies are now available that attest to the breadth of dysfunction of conduct-disordered children as they mature into adulthood. Table 3.1 highlights the characteristics that these children are likely to evince when they become adults.

Even though conduct disorder in childhood portends a number of other significant problems in adulthood, not all antisocial children suffer impairment as adults. Nevertheless, data suggest that a high percentage of children are likely to suffer as adults. Across several different samples, Robins (1978) noted that among the most severely antisocial children, fewer than 50% became antisocial adults. Even though fewer than half of the children continue antisocial behavior into adulthood, the percentage is still quite high.

If diverse diagnoses are considered, rather than serious antisocial behavior alone, the picture of impairment in adulthood is much worse. Among children referred for antisocial behavior, 84% received a diagnosis of psychiatric disorder as adults (Robins, 1966). Although these diagnoses vary in degree of impairment (e.g., psychoses, neuroses), the data suggest that the majority of children with clinically referred antisocial behavior will suffer from a significant degree of impairment as adults. Thus, the prognosis is relatively poor considering only subsequent psychiatric impairment. Such impairment obviously is likely to correlate with performance in other spheres (see Table 3.1).

As noted above, not all antisocial youths become antisocial adults. As with the onset of antisocial behaviors, several risk factors for continuation of these behaviors have been identified. Major factors that influence whether antisocial youths are likely to continue their behavior into adulthood are summarized in Table 3.2. The factors are only highlighted here in part because they resemble those factors discussed in relation to the onset of antisocial behavior. As in the earlier discussion, the complexity of prognosticators is not fully conveyed by merely enumerating individual risk factors. For example, the risk for a long-term antisocial behavior in adulthood is increased when the father has a history of antisocial behavior and alcoholism, as noted in Table 3.2; this risk is increased when both the father and mother have been antisocial and alcoholic. However, when the mother alone shows these characteristics, the child is not at increased risk for antisocial personality (Robins, 1966). Thus, within a given variable, and among alternative variables, the relationships may be relatively complex.

Among the many different variables that might be listed, it is important to underscore those that account for the major sources of variance in predicting long-term outcome. Research has suggested that the prediction of antisocial behavior in adulthood is more related to the child's history of antisocial behavior rather than parent, family, and socioeconomic factors (Hanson et al., 1984; Huesmann et al., 1984; Robins, 1978). Early onset of antisocial behaviors, antisocial acts evident across multiple settings (e.g., home and school), and many and diverse antisocial behaviors (e.g., several versus few, covert and overt acts) are the primary factors that predict untoward long-term consequences (Loeber & Dishion, 1983; Rutter & Giller, 1983).

Table 3.2 Characteristics that Predict Continued Antisocial Behavior in Adulthood

Characteristic	*Specific Pattern*
1. Age of Onset	Earlier onset (e.g., before 10 or 12) of their antisocial behavior. Early onset also is related to rate and seriousness of later antisocial behavior
2. Breadth of Deviance	A greater number of different types of antisocial behaviors; a greater variety of situations in which antisocial behavior is manifest (e.g., at home, school); a greater range of persons or organizations against whom such behaviors are expressed
3. Frequency of Antisocial Behavior	A greater number of different antisocial episodes independently of whether they include a number of different behaviors
4. Seriousness of the Behavior	Relatively serious antisocial behavior in childhood, especially if the behavior could be grounds for adjudication
5. Type of Symptoms	The following specific antisocial behaviors: lying, impulsiveness, truancy, running away, theft, and staying out late. Also, if they show nonantisocial symptoms of slovenliness and enuresis (after age 6)
6. Parent Characteristics	Parent psychopathology, particularly if antisocial behavior; father has record of arrest, unemployment, alcoholism; poor parental supervision of child; overly strict, lax or inconsistent discipline
7. Family	Greater if from homes with marital discord and larger family size

NOTE: These characteristics are based on comparisons of clinically referred children identified for antisocial behavior relative to control clinic referrals or normal controls or from comparisons of delinquent and nondelinquent youths (see Farrington, 1978; Glueck & Glueck, 1950; Hamparian, Schuster, Dinitz, & Conrad, 1978; Hanson et al., 1984; Loeber, 1982; Mitchell & Rosa, 1981; Robins, 1966, 1978; Robins & Ratcliff, 1979; Wolfgang et al., 1972).

CAUSES OF ANTISOCIAL BEHAVIOR

Two related questions emerge from the study of risk factors. First, to what extent is antisocial behavior influenced by genetic, environmental, or combined factors? Many factors that place the child at risk for antisocial behavior could be due to hereditary and/or environmental influences. For example, antisocial behavior in the parent may lead to antisocial behavior in the child through direct operation of an inherited factor or through modeling, poor child-rearing practices, or their combination.

Second, what are the specific mechanisms through which antisocial behaviors emerge? If genetic or environmental influences are shown to play a role in antisocial behavior, this does not resolve precisely how the influence leads to specific antisocial behaviors. For example, harsh and inconsistent parent discipline practices are associated with antisocial behavior, but through what intervening processes? Evidence has addressed both of the above questions.

Gene-Environment Influences

Several lines of evidence have emerged in support of the role of genetic factors. *Twin studies* are frequently used to demonstrate the role of genetic influences because monozygotic twins are, of course, much more similar genetically than dizygotic twins. If there is a genetic factor expressed in one monozygotic twin, the chances of it occurring in the other twin would be expected to be higher than if the same phenomenon occurred in dizygotic twins. In fact, twin studies have shown greater concordance of criminality and antisocial behavior among monozygotic rather than dizygotic twins (e.g., Christiansen, 1974; Cloninger, Christiansen, Reich, & Gottesman, 1978). Attribution of the differences in concordance between monozygotic and dizygotic twins to genetic factors assumes that the environments for different types of twins are equated. Yet, environmental factors may be more similar for monozygotic than for dizygotic twins (Christiansen, 1974).

Adoption studies better separate genetic and environmental influences because the child often is separated from the biological parent at birth. Adoption studies have shown that antisocial behavior and criminality in the offspring are more likely when the biological relative has shown such behavior than when the relative has not (e.g., Cadoret, 1978; Crowe, 1974). The relatively frequent replication of the increased risk due to antisocial behavior in the biological parent of adoptees establishes the role of genetics in accounting for some portion of variance in the emergence of conduct disorder. Yet, genetic factors alone cannot account for current findings. For example, criminality aggregates among siblings in the home more often than can be readily explained by genetic factors (Cloninger, Reich, & Guze, 1975). Adoption studies have also affirmed the influence of such environmental factors as adverse conditions in the home (e.g., marital discord, psychiatric dysfunction), exposure to discontinuous mothering before being placed in the final adoptive setting and the age at which the child has been adopted (Cadoret & Cain, 1981; Crowe, 1974; Hutchings & Mednick, 1975). This work suggests the combined role of genetic and environmental factors.

The dual contribution of genetic and environmental influences can be seen in studies that show that antisocial behavior in both the biological and adoptive parent increases the risk of antisocial behavior in the child (Mednick & Hutchings, 1978), although the impact of the biological parent is much greater. Other studies examining a number of variables have shown that the risk is greatly increased when both genetic and environmental influences are present (e.g., Cadoret, Caine, & Crowe, 1983; Cloninger, Sigvardsson, Bohman, & von Knorring, 1982). Yet, there are important nuances showing the interaction of genetic and environmental factors with other variables.

For example, gender of the child has been shown to interact with the influence of genetic and environmental factors. In studies of adoptees, Cadoret and Cain (1980, 1981) found that having an alcoholic biological relative, adverse home conditions in the adoptive home, and discontinuous mothering predicted antisocial behavior in adolescent males. However, for female adolescents, only having an antisocial or mentally retarded biological parent predicted antisocial behavior. Thus, environmental factors (home conditions and mothering practices) only emerged as predictors for males suggesting their greater susceptibility to environmental influences. Other studies have suggested differences in vulnerability of males and females to environmental factors (e.g., divorce or institutional care) that may place the child at risk for antisocial behavior, although many of the influences appear to be a matter of degree rather than an all-or-none phenomenon (Cloninger, Reich, & Guze, 1978; Rutter, 1972; Wolkind & Rutter, 1973). Variables other than gender have been found to mediate the influence of genetic and/or environmental factors on antisocial behavior. For example, the expression of genetic influences for antisocial behavior appears to be greater for women, persons of higher socioeconomic class, and persons in areas where criminality is relatively infrequent (e.g., rural areas) (Christiansen, 1974).

Mechanisms Through Which Genetic and/or Environmental Factors Operate

Establishing the role of genetic and environmental factors does not, by itself, elaborate the specific mechanisms through which such factors operate. For example, the presence of antisocial behavior or alcoholism in a biological relative may predispose the child to antisocial behavior but this does not explain exactly how antisocial behavior is influenced. Neurohumors, hormones, altered thresholds in response to provocation or any number of anatomical and physiological correlates might mediate behavioral patterns, each of which is consistent with a genetic component.

An extraordinarily large number of mechanisms that promote or cause antisocial behavior and criminality have been proposed. Indeed, multiple views have emerged from each of the many disciplines that lay claim to the problem (for instance, sociology, psychology, psychiatry, biology, and others (see Hippchen, 1978; Lewis, 1981; Rutter & Giller, 1983; Shaffer, Meyer-Bahlburg, & Stokman, 1981). A few views are worth highlighting that are consistent with genetic and environmental factors mentioned earlier.

Several studies have attempted to identify biological factors that distinguish individuals with antisocial behavior (see Hare 1978; Mednick & Christiansen, 1977). Such factors, if identified, might suggest conditions that are transmitted genetically. At one time, the view was proposed and widely publicized that violent behavior could be accounted for by *chromosomal abnormalities* (XYY syndrome in males). However, this view has been rejected with evidence that the syndrome is infrequent and not evident in the vast majority of cases of violent behavior or criminality (Mednick & Hutchings, 1978).

Many studies of antisocial behavior have focused on *biochemical differences*. For example, using a small sample of aggressive adults (with personality disorders), altered serotonin metabolism (lower CSF 5-hydroxyindoleacetic acid [5-HIAA]) was associated with aggressive and suicidal behavior (Brown et al., 1982). Other researchers have identified higher levels of plasma testosterone among violent delinquents compared to normal controls (Mattsson, Schalling, Olwens, Low, & Svensson, 1980). Moreover, among normals, plasma testosterone is positively correlated with low frustration tolerance and self-reports of verbal and physical aggression, particularly in response to provocation and threat (Olweus, Mattsson, Schalling, & Low,

1980). However, testosterone was not found to be related to antisocial behaviors such as theft, truancy, and property destruction. A few studies have found low serum cholesterol to be associated with habitually aggressive behavior in adolescents and adults (Virkkunen, 1983; Virkkunen & Penttinen, 1984). The basis for the differences is unclear at present. Given that cholesterol is implicated in glucose and fat metabolism, the range of potential mechanisms (e.g., neurohumors, hormone secretion) is vast.

Research occasionally has found biochemical differences associated with subtypes of antisocial behavior. For example, socialized and undersocialized conduct disorder children evince enzyme differences that mediate neurotransmitters, for instance, dopamine *B*-hydroxylase (DHB), catechol O-methyltransferase (COMT) (Rogeness, Hernandez, Macedo, & Mitchell, 1982). Apart from biochemical differences, other biological correlates of antisocial behavior have been noted. As mentioned earlier, seizures and other neurological abnormalities occasionally have been found to distinguish antisocial youths (Lewis et al., 1979, 1983). Biochemical and neurological differences suggest possible factors that might genetically influence behavior but the mechanisms leading to antisocial behaviors are still not clear or well tied to theories that predict conduct disorder rather than psychiatric impairment in general. Nevertheless, research of this ilk carries one step further the study of biological mechanisms that might underlie forms of antisocial behavior.

Other biological factors have been evaluated as possible causal agents (McCord, 1982). For example, Mednick (1975, 1978) has suggested that inherited *arousal patterns* of the autonomic nervous system may influence the extent to which antisocial persons fail to learn to inhibit antisocial behavior through fear reduction and reduced arousal (see Mednick, 1978). The view incorporates influences that can be traced to heredity (psychophysiological arousal) and environment (learning experiences).

Several mechanisms have been proposed that focus on nonbiological or environmental factors that lead to the emergence of antisocial behavior. Prominent among such factors has been the *role of child-parent interaction* where aggressive behavior is fostered in the child (Patterson, 1982). Research has firmly established that parents of antisocial (especially aggressive) children inadvertently promote antisocial behavior by pervasively poor parenting skills. Compared to parents of nonclinic children, these parents punish inconsistently but quite frequently and ineffectively, attend to and reward inappropriate child behavior, and reinforce extremely coercive and aversive child behavior (yelling and screaming).

Another view that focuses on nonbiological factors nicely integrates findings on cognitive and social processes leading to antisocial behavior in children. Dodge (1985) has conducted a series of studies that has identified a significant *attributional bias* among aggressive children. Such children tend to view ambiguous situations (when the intention of others is not clear) as hostile. The perception of hostility helps to precipitate aggressive acts that are merely retaliatory from the standpoint of the aggressive child. These acts, however, do not seem justified in the views of his peers. Peer rejection of the aggressive child appears to follow aggressive behavior. The reactions of the peers and their dislike of and isolation from the aggressive child provide additional cues to the aggressive child that the environment is hostile. Thus, a vicious circle of aggressive behavior and untoward peer reactions can be sustained and accelerated. Related views have identified deficits in a number of specific cognitive processes that underlie social behavior in aggressive children (Spivack, Platt, & Shure, 1976).

In general, the mechanisms that may be involved in antisocial behavior have received scant empirical attention. There are obvious obstacles for theory and research in this area. No single theory is likely to account for the emergence of the full range of antisocial behaviors. The vast area may need to be viewed from the standpoint of subtypes of behaviors, individuals, and environments so that minitheories can be developed and tested. At the very least, progress on the mechanisms through which specific types of antisocial behaviors emerge will require integration of advances in diagnosis and identification of risk factors.

SUMMARY AND CONCLUSIONS

Several factors have been identified that place a child at risk for conduct disorder. Early signs of troublesome or obstreperous behavior at home or at school are salient predictors. In addition, a variety of parent and family characteristics have been identified as risk factors including criminality, antisocial behavior, and alcoholism in the parents, marital discord, and harsh and inconsistent discipline practices, among others.

Along with the study of risk factors, research has explored the joint contributions of heredity and environment. Twin and adoption studies have affirmed not only the importance of genetic influences but also the fact that such influences interact with a variety of environmental, subject, and demographic variables. A difficulty in discussing conduct disorder, identifying risk factors, and testing etiological hypotheses pertains to the breadth of the behaviors and populations that are encompassed. The problem of heterogeneity of the population and their characteristics plagues diverse facets of the literature including epidemiological, diagnostic, treatment, and other kinds of studies.

The study of risk factors, onset and clinical course has revealed the remarkable stability and continuity of antisocial behavior. Not only is there continuity of antisocial behavior from childhood through adolescence and adulthood but also a transgenerational continuation. Both adoption studies and studies of dysfunction in parents and grandparents of antisocial youths have helped to establish the continuity across generations. Although the precise bases for this continuity (i.e., extent to which particular gene-action models apply, the influence of socioenvironmental factors) are not well established, the fact that conduct disorder generally has a continuous course is noteworthy. The stability and continuity of conduct disorder mean that interventions designed to ameliorate these behaviors are quite important. The next chapters review and evaluate alternative treatment and preventive techniques.

4

CURRENT TREATMENTS

Antisocial youths are likely to evince a broad range of dysfunctions in their social behaviors, academic performance, and cognitive processes, in addition to their conduct problem behaviors (e.g., aggressive acts). They also are likely to live with parents who evince dysfunction of their own (e.g., psychopathology, marital discord). Given the array of dysfunctions that the child and family are likely to present, the focus of almost any particular therapeutic approach (e.g., intrapsychic or cognitive processes of the child, communication or child-rearing patterns of the parents) might be readily justified. It is no surprise that many different types of treatments currently are available. The purpose of the present chapter is to convey the range of treatment approaches that are currently in use and to discuss alternative approaches that show particular promise.[1]

OVERVIEW OF CURRENT TREATMENTS

Many different classes of treatment can be identified. The majority of treatments in current use focus on the *individual* child or adolescent. The treatments are directed at altering a particular facet of functioning or processes within the identified patient. Diverse approaches focus on changing the individual child including individual and group therapy, behavioral and cognitive therapies, and pharmacotherapies. A number of other treatments focus on changing the *family*. With these treatments, the problem of the antisocial youth is viewed in the context of processes within the family. Treatment is aimed at altering interactional patterns in the home. Techniques such as family therapy and parent management training are examples.

Other treatments are worth delineating on the basis of their use or incorporation of therapeutic influences in the context of the *community*. Direct contact and involvement of youth with prosocial peers and community services are accorded major weight. Community-based techniques often rely on other treatments such as psychotherapy and behavior therapy. Yet, these are integrated within a larger social, organizational, and peer-group context.

There are many different techniques within these broad classes. Table 4.1 highlights major classes of treatment and their therapeutic focus. Within a given type of treatment, several variations can be identified. For example, individual psychotherapy consists of psychodynamic, nondirective, play therapies, and others. Similarly, behavior therapy can include a range of techniques such as social skills training, contingency management, and token economies. At the level of specific techniques, rather than the more generic classes of treatment, the number of procedures would be large.

The plethora of available techniques might be viewed as a healthy sign that the field has not become rigidly set on one or two techniques. On the other hand, the diversity of available procedures suggests that no particular approach has been shown to ameliorate antisocial behavior. Although there are many different techniques, relatively little well-controlled outcome evidence can be presented on their behalf (see Kazdin, 1985). At present, no treatment has been clearly shown to ameliorate conduct disorder and to controvert the untoward consequences to which it often leads. A few techniques have been carefully investigated in controlled trials. Four techniques in particular appear to be especially promising: parent management training, functional family therapy, problem-solving skills training, and community-based treatment.

HIGHLY PROMISING APPROACHES

Parent Management Training

Background and Underlying Rationale. Parent management training (PMT) refers to procedures in which a parent or parents are trained to interact differently with their child. Training is based on the general

Table 4.1 Therapeutic Focus and Processes of Major Classes of Treatment for Antisocial Behavior

Types of Treatment	*Focus*	*Key Processes*
Child-Focused Treatments		
Individual Psychotherapy	Focus on intrapsychic bases of antisocial behavior especially conflicts and psychological processes that were adversely affected over the course of development.	Relationship with the therapist is the primary medium through which change is achieved. Treatment provides a corrective emotional experience by providing insight and exploring new ways of behaving.
Group Psychotherapy	Processes of individual therapy, as noted above. Additional processes are reassurance, feedback, and vicarious gains by peers. Group processes such as cohesion, leadership also serve as the focus.	Relationship with the therapist and peers as part of the group. Group processes emerge to provide children with experiences and feelings of others and opportunities to test their own views and behaviors.
Behavior Therapy	Problematic behaviors presented as target symptoms or behaviors designed to controvert these symptoms (e.g., prosocial behaviors).	Learning of new behaviors through direct training, via modeling, reinforcement, practice and role playing. Training in the situations (e.g., at home, in the community) where the problematic behaviors occur.
Problem-Solving Skills Training	Cognitive processes and interpersonal cognitive problem-solving skills that underlie social behavior.	Teach problem-solving skills to children by engaging in a step-by-step approach to interpersonal situations. Use of modeling, practice, rehearsal and role play to develop problem-solving skills. Development of an internal dialogue or private speech that utilizes the processes of identifying prosocial solutions to problems.

Table 4.1 Continued

Pharmacotherapy	Designed to affect the biological substrates of behavior, especially in light of laboratory-based findings on neurohumors, biological cycles, and other physiological correlates of aggressive and emotional behavior.	Administration of psychotropic agents to control antisocial behavior. Lithium carbonate and haloperidol have been used because of their anti-aggressive effects.
Residential Treatments	Means of administrating other techniques in day treatment or residential setting. Foci of other techniques apply.	Processes of other techniques apply. Also, separation of the child from parents or removal from the home situation may help reduce untoward processes or crises that contribute to the clinical problem.
Family-Focused Treatments		
Family Therapy	Family as a functioning system serves as focus rather than the identified patient. Interpersonal relationships, organization, roles, and dynamics of the family.	Communication, relationships, and structure within the family and processes as autonomy, problem solving, and negotiation.
Parent Management Training	Interactions in the home, especially those involving coercive exchanges.	Direct training of parents to develop prosocial behavior in their children. Explicit use of social learning techniques to influence the child.
Community-Based Treatments		
Community-wide Interventions	Focus on activities and community programs to foster competence and peer relations.	Develop prosocial behavior and connections with peers. Activities are seen to promote prosocial behavior and to be incompatible with antisocial behavior.

view that conduct problem behavior is inadvertently developed and sustained in the home by maladaptive parent-child interactions. In fact, research has shown that parents of antisocial youths engage in several practices that promote aggressive behavior and suppress prosocial behavior. These practices include directly reinforcing deviant behavior, frequently and ineffectively using commands and harsh punishment, and failing to attend to appropriate behavior (Patterson, 1982).

Coercive interaction patterns in particular play a central role in promoting aggressive child behavior. *Coercion* refers to deviant behavior on the part of one person (e.g., the child) that is rewarded by another person (e.g., the parent). Aggressive children are inadvertently rewarded for their aggressive interactions and their escalation of coercive behaviors. The general purpose of PMT is to alter the pattern of interchanges between parent and child so that prosocial rather than coercive behavior is directly reinforced and supported within the family. This requires developing several different parenting behaviors such as establishing the rules for the child to follow, providing positive reinforcement for appropriate behavior, delivering mild forms of punishment to suppress behavior, negotiating compromises, and other procedures.[2]

Characteristics of Treatment. Although many variations of PMT exist, several common characteristics can be identified. First, treatment is conducted primarily with the parents who directly implement several procedures in the home. There usually is no direct intervention of the therapist with the child. Second, parents are trained to identify, define, and observe problem behavior in new ways. The careful specification of the problem is essential for the delivery of reinforcing or punishing consequences and for evaluating if the program is working.

Third, the treatment sessions cover social learning principles and the procedures that follow from them. Considerable time is devoted to such techniques as positive reinforcement (e.g., the use of social praise and tokens or points for prosocial behavior), mild punishment (e.g., use of time out from reinforcement, loss of privileges), negotiation, contingency contracting, and other procedures. Fourth, the sessions provide opportunities for parents to see how the techniques are implemented, to practice using the techniques, and to review the behavior change programs in the home. The therapist uses instructions, modeling, role-playing, and rehearsal to convey how the techniques are implemented.

The immediate goal of the program is to develop specific skills in the parents. This is usually achieved by having parents apply their skills to relatively simple behaviors that can be easily observed and that are not enmeshed with more provoking interactions (e.g., punishment, battles of the will, coercive interchanges). As the parents become more proficient, the focus of the program can address the child's most severely problematic behaviors and encompass other problem areas (e.g., school behavior).

Overview of the Outcome Evidence. Parent management training has been evaluated in hundreds of outcome studies with behavior problem children varying in age and degree of severity of dysfunction (see Kazdin, 1985). The work of Patterson and his colleagues, spanning two decades, exemplifies the outcome research on parent training with antisocial youths. Over 200 families have been seen that include primarily aggressive children (ages 3 to 12 years) referred for outpatient treatment (see Patterson, 1982). The effectiveness of treatment has been evaluated on parent and teacher reports of deviant behavior as well as direct observation of child behavior at home and at school.

Several controlled studies have demonstrated marked improvements in child behavior over the course of treatment. Moreover, these changes surpass those achieved with variations of family-based psychotherapy, attention-placebo (discussion) and no-treatment conditions (Patterson et al., 1982; Walter & Gilmore, 1973; Wiltz & Patterson, 1974). The effects of treatment have also been shown to bring the problematic behaviors of treated children within normative levels of their peers who are functioning adequately (Eyberg & Johnson, 1974; Patterson, 1974; Wells, Forehand, & Griest, 1980). Follow-up assessment has shown that the gains are often maintained one year after treatment (e.g., Fleischman & Szykula, 1981); longer follow-up periods have shown the continued benefits of treatment up to 4.5 years later (Baum & Forehand, 1981).

The impact of PMT is relatively broad. To begin with, the effects of treatment are evident for child behaviors that have not been focused on directly as part of training. Also, siblings improve, even though they are not directly focused on in treatment. In addition, maternal psychopathology, particularly depression, has been shown to decrease systematically following PMT. These changes suggest that PMT alters multiple aspects of dysfunctional families (see Kazdin, 1985; Moreland, Schwebel, Beck, & Wells, 1982; Patterson & Fleischman, 1979).

Factors that Contribute to Outcome. Several characteristics of the treatment and the families who participate contribute to treatment outcome. Among the treatment characteristics, duration of treatment appears to influence outcome. Brief and time-limited treatments (e.g., less than 10 hrs) are less likely to show benefits with clinical populations. More dramatic and durable effects have been achieved with protracted or time unlimited programs extending up to 50 or 60 hours of treatment (see Kazdin, 1985). Second, specific training components such as providing parents with in-depth knowledge of social learning principles and utilizing time out from reinforcement in the home enhance treatment effects (e.g., McMahon, Forehand, & Griest, 1981; Wahler & Fox, 1980). Third, some evidence suggests that therapist training and skill are associated with the magnitude and durability of therapeutic changes (Fleischman, 1982; Patterson, 1974), although this has yet to be carefully tested.

Parent and family characteristics also relate to treatment outcome. As might be expected, families characterized by many risk factors associated with childhood dysfunction (e.g., marital discord and parent psychopathology) tend to show fewer gains in treatment than families without these characteristics (e.g., Strain, Young, & Horowitz, 1981). Moreover, when gains are achieved in treatment, they are unlikely to be maintained in families with socioeconomic disadvantages.

The social support system of the mother outside of the home also contributes to the efficacy of PMT (Dumas & Wahler, 1983). Mothers who are insulated from social supports outside the home (i.e., have few positive social contacts with relatives and friends) are less likely to profit from treatment. Thus, variables beyond the specific parent-child interactions need to be considered in treatment. In fact, one study found that when PMT addresses many of the family problems (e.g., parental adjustment, marital adjustment, and extrafamilial relations), the efficacy of treatment in terms of child behavior change is enhanced (Griest et al., 1982).

Overall Evaluation. Several features of PMT make it one of the more promising treatments for conduct disorders. First, the treatment has been shown to be effective with conduct problem children varying in severity of clinical dysfunction. Treatment effects have been shown to be maintained up to one year and occasionally longer. Moreover, changes at home and at school have been shown to bring deviant behavior of treated children within the range of children functioning normally. Second, the benefits of treatment often extend beyond the target child. For example, siblings have been shown to profit from PMT. This may be an important advantage because siblings of antisocial youths are at risk for antisocial behavior (Twito & Stewart, 1982).

Third, along with outcome investigations, basic research has been conducted on family interaction patterns and influences outside of the home that may have impact on treatment outcome. This research is likely not only to contribute directly to improved treatment outcomes but also to enhance our understanding of the emergence of antisocial behavior. Fourth, a major advantage is the availability of treatment manuals and training materials for parents and professional therapists (see Ollendick & Cerny, 1981, for a list). The extensive materials make this modality of treatment potentially widely available.

Several limitations of PMT can be identified as well. First, some families may not respond to treatment. Explicit procedures may need to be included in treatment to address family and parent conflict that influence the parent-child interactions in the home. Second, PMT makes several demands on the parents such as mastering educational materials that convey major principles underlying the program, systematically observing deviant child behavior and implementing specific procedures at home, attending weekly sessions, and responding to frequent telephone contacts made by the therapist. For some families, the demands may be too great to continue in treatment. Third and related, for many antisocial children, PMT is simply not a viable option. PMT requires at least one parent who is available, willing, and capable of following through with treatment. Some parents cannot participate because of their own dysfunction; others will not participate because they feel they have reached their limits in trying to help their child.

Many questions about the effects of PMT remain to be addressed. For example, few reports have included antisocial adolescents. This population may be less readily influenced by the rewarding and punishing consequences that parents can apply in the home. Also, different types of antisocial children may not respond equally well to treatment. For example, preliminary evidence suggests that aggressive children respond better than do children whose problems are primarily nonaggressive (e.g., stealing, truancy) (Patterson, 1982). The interaction of treatment with child and family characteristics needs to be investigated more systematically. On balance, PMT is one of the most promising treatment modalities. No other intervention for antisocial children has been investigated as thoroughly as PMT and has shown as favorable results.

Functional Family Therapy

Background and Underlying Rationale. Functional family therapy (FFT) reflects an integrative approach to treatment that relies upon systems theory and behaviorism (Alexander & Parsons, 1982; Barton & Alexander, 1981). Clinical problems are conceptualized from the standpoint of the functions they serve in the family as a system, as well as for individual family members. The assumption is made that the problem behavior evident in the child is the only way that some interpersonal functions (e.g., intimacy, distancing, support) can be met among family members. Maladaptive processes within the family are considered to preclude a more direct means of fulfilling these functions. The goal of treatment is to alter interaction and communication patterns in such a way as to foster more adaptive functioning.

The underlying rationale emphasizes a family systems approach. The rationale for specific treatment strategies, as they relate to antisocial child behavior, draws upon the behavioral family interaction literature that has helped to identify specific maladaptive parent-child (e.g., coercive) interactions (Patterson, 1982). FFT views interaction patterns from a broader systems view than the somewhat more molecular view underlying parent management training. Research underlying FFT has found that families of delinquents show higher rates of defensiveness in their communications, both in parent-child and parent-parent interactions, and also lower rates of mutual support compared to families of nondelinquents (Alexander, 1973). Improving these communication and support functions is a goal of treatment.

Characteristics of Treatment. FFT requires that the family see the clinical problem from the relational functions it serves within the family. The therapist points out interdependencies and contingencies between family members in their day-to-day functioning and with specific reference to the problem that has served as the basis for seeking treatment. Once the family sees alternative ways of viewing the problem, the incentive for interacting more constructively is increased.

The main goals of treatment are to increase reciprocity and positive reinforcement among family members, to establish clear communication, to help specify behaviors that family members desire from each other, to negotiate constructively, and to help identify solutions to interpersonal problems. The family members read a manual that describes behavioral principles (e.g., reinforcement and extinction) to develop familiarity with the concepts used in treatment. In therapy, family members identify behaviors they would like others to perform. Responses are incorporated into a reinforcement system in the home to promote adaptive behavior in exchange for privileges. However, the primary focus is within the treatment sessions where family communication patterns are altered directly. During the sessions, the therapist provides social reinforcement (verbal and nonverbal praise) for communications that suggest solutions to problems, provide information to clarify problems, or offer feedback to other family members.

Outcome Evidence. Only a few studies of FFT have been reported. These have produced relatively clear effects. The initial study included male and female delinquent adolescents referred to juvenile court for a variety of behaviors such as running away, truancy, theft, and unmanageability (Parsons & Alexander, 1973). Cases were assigned to the family therapy approach noted above, to an attention-placebo condition (group discussion and expression of feeling), or to a no-treatment control group. Posttreatment evaluation, following eight treatment sessions, revealed that the family therapy condition led to greater discussion among family members, that family members spoke more equitably, and that frequency and duration of spontaneous speech increased. The changes were significantly greater than in the attention-placebo and no-treatment groups.

In an extension of the above program, Alexander and Parsons (1973) compared FFT, client-centered family groups, psychodynamically oriented family therapy, and no treatment. The results indicated greater improvement on family interaction measures and lower recidivism rates from juvenile court records up to 18 months after treatment for the FFT group. Follow-up data obtained 2½ years later, indicated that the siblings of those who received FFT showed significantly lower rates of referral to juvenile courts (Klein, Alexander & Parsons, 1977). Thus, the results suggest significant changes on both index children as well as their siblings.

Overall Evaluation. Given the above outcome studies, functional family therapy shows obvious promise. Additional replications are needed. Albeit few studies exist, already some important statements can be made about the treatment. First, the effectiveness of treatment is influenced by the relationship (e.g., warmth, integration of affect and behavior) and structuring (e.g., directiveness) skills of the therapist (Alexander, Barton, Schiavo, & Parsons, 1976). Second, process measures of family interactions at posttreatment are related to subsequent recidivism (Alexander & Parsons, 1973). This finding adds credence to the model from which treatment was derived. Finally, in the outcome studies, client-centered and psychodynamically oriented forms of family-based therapies have not achieved the positive effects of FFT. Thus, treatment of the problem at the level of the family per se does not appear to be sufficient to alter antisocial behavior.

Cognitive Problem-Solving Skills Training

Background and Underlying Rationale. Problem-solving skills training (PSST) focuses on the child's cognitive processes (perceptions, self-statements, attributions, expectations, and problem-solving skills) that are presumed to underlie maladaptive behavior. The assumption of PSST is that children with deviant behavior suffer deficiencies in particular processes or from an inability to use or apply cognitive skills.[3]

Cognitive processes have been frequently accorded a major role in conduct problems such as aggressive behavior (Berkowitz, 1977; Novaco, 1978). Aggression is not merely triggered by environmental events but rather through the way in which these events are perceived and processed. The processing refers to the child's appraisals of the situation, anticipated reactions of others, and self-statements in response to particular events. Psychiatric inpatient children and school children identified as aggressive have shown a predisposition to attribute hostile intent to others, especially in social situations where the cues of actual intent are ambiguous (Dodge, 1985). Understandably, when situations are initially perceived as hostile, children are more likely to react aggressively.

The ability to take the perspective of, or to empathize with, other persons is also related to aggressive behavior. For example, among delinquents, those who are aggressive (i.e., committed acts against other persons or property) are less empathic than nonaggressive delinquents (see Ellis, 1982). Perspective taking appears to increase with age among normal children and adolescents and to be inversely related to the expression of aggression (Feshbach, 1975).

The relation between cognitive processes and behavioral adjustment has been evaluated extensively by Spivack and Shure (1982; Shure & Spivack, 1978; Spivack et al., 1976). These investigators have identified different cognitive processes or interpersonal cognitive problem-solving skills that underlie social behavior. These processes include the following:

(1) *Alternative Solution Thinking*—the ability to generate different options (solutions) that can solve problems in interpersonal situations.
(2) *Means-End Thinking*—awareness of the intermediate steps required to achieve a particular goal.
(3) *Consequential Thinking*—the ability to identify what might happen as a direct result of acting in a particular way or choosing a particular solution.
(4) *Causal Thinking*—the ability to relate one event to another over time and to understand why one event led to a particular action of other persons.
(5) *Sensitivity to Interpersonal Problems*—the ability to perceive a problem when it exists and to identify the interpersonal aspects of the confrontation that may emerge.

The ability to engage in the above problem-solving steps is related to behavioral adjustment, as measured in teacher ratings of acting out behavior and social withdrawal. Disturbed children tend to generate fewer alternative solutions to interpersonal problems, to focus on ends or goals rather than the intermediate steps to obtain them, to see fewer consequences associated with their behavior, to fail to recognize the causes of other people's behavior, and to be less sensitive to interpersonal conflict (Spivack et al., 1976).

Characteristics of Treatment. Many variations of PSST have emerged for conduct problem children (Camp & Bash, 1985; Kendall & Braswell, 1985; Spivack et al., 1976). The variations share many characteristics. First, the emphasis is on *how* the child approaches situations. Although it is obviously important that the child ultimately select appropriate means of behaving in every day life, the primary focus is on the thought *processes* rather than the *outcome* or specific behavioral acts that result. Second, the treatment attempts to teach the child to engage in a step-by-step approach to solve problems. The method is usually achieved by having the child make statements (self-instructions) to himself or herself that direct attention to certain aspects of the problem or tasks that lead to effective solutions. Third, treatment utilizes structured tasks involving games, academic activities, and stories. Over the course of treatment, the cognitive problem-solving skills are increasingly applied to real-life situations.

Fourth, the therapist usually plays an active role in treatment. The therapist models the cognitive processes by making verbal self-statements, applies the sequence of statements to particular problems, provides cues to the child to prompt use of the skills, and delivers feedback and praise to develop correct use of the skills. Finally, treatment usually combines several different procedures including modeling and practice, role-playing, and reinforcement and mild punishment (loss of points or tokens).

Overview of the Outcome Evidence. A number of researchers have conducted programmatic series of studies showing the efficacy of PSST (see Kendall & Braswell, 1985; Spivack & Shure, 1982). Research has established the efficacy of alternative variations of treatment. The majority of studies, however, have evaluated the impact of training on cognitive processes and laboratory-task performance, rather than deviant child behavior (see Gresham, 1985; Kazdin, 1985). Spivack and others (1976) have demonstrated with different age groups that developing interpersonal problem-solving skills leads to improved ratings of behavioral adjustment in the classroom as well as increased interpersonal attributes such as popularity and likeability. Relatively few studies have evaluated PSST with clinical samples referred because of conduct disorder. Studies of aggressive children and adolescents have shown that cognitively based treatment can lead to significant changes in behavior at home, at school, and in the community and that these gains are evident up to one year later (Arbuthnot & Gordon, 1986; Lochman, Burch, Curry, & Lampron, 1984). Yet, the bulk of the evidence has focused on "impulsive" children who show problems of self-control (Kendall & Braswell, 1985). Further trials are clearly warranted.

Few studies have elaborated the factors that contribute to treatment outcome. Some evidence has suggested that the greater the level of child aggression, the less effective treatment is (Kendall & Braswell, 1985). Duration of treatment, age, and cognitive development have been suggested as potential influences (Cole & Kazdin, 1980). These have yet to be explored in the context of treatment trials.

Overall Evaluation. PSST at this point in time has not been shown to be an effective treatment for antisocial behavior. Nevertheless, several features make this one of the more promising psychosocial approaches to the problem. First, PSST is tied to theory and research in developmental psychology. Theory and research on the emergence and maturation of cognitive processes and the relation of these processes to adjustment provide an important foundation for generating and testing treatment techniques. Also, maladaptive cognitive processes has been shown to relate to other variables (e.g., parents' child-rearing practices) that are correlated with the development and maintenance of antisocial behavior (Shure & Spivack, 1978).

Second, developmental differences may need to be considered in designing effective treatments. Processes highly significant at one age (e.g., means-ends thinking in adolescents) may be less critical at other ages, such as early childhood (Spivack et al., 1976). Third, rigorous evidence attests to the fact that PSST can produce change in children with mild adjustment problems. That change is achieved at all and that these changes cannot be attributed to such influences as exposure to specific tasks or stimulus materials and discussion of interpersonal situations, should not be treated lightly. Fourth, a major feature of PSST for both purposes of clinical application and research is that variations of the approach are available in manual form (e.g., Camp

& Bash, 1985; Kendall & Braswell, 1985; Spivack et al., 1976). Specification of treatment procedures in manual form helps promote further research on the efficacy of treatment.

There are clear limitations to the application of PSST as well. Research to date has generally adopted the view that children with problems of adjustment, broadly conceived, have cognitive deficits. There has been little attempt to relate specific cognitive deficits to particular types of clinical dysfunction. For example, Spivack and others (1976) have found similar cognitive deficits of children who are socially withdrawn or who act out. Their work with adolescents and adults has also shown that drug addicts, delinquents, and schizophrenic patients evince cognitive deficits compared to normals matched on various demographic variables. Finer distinctions need to be explored to delineate the cognitive correlates or underpinnings of specific clinical problems.

Evaluating the clinical efficacy of PSST is impeded by the frequent failure of outcome studies to delineate the population that is treated. Few studies have utilized stringent selection criteria or have described the sample well enough to instill confidence that the children were severely impaired and that the application of treatment was related to the nature of the impairment. Existing studies show that various forms of PSST can produce relatively consistent changes on a variety of measures that reflect cognitive style, thought processes, perception, aspects of intelligence, and academic performance. Additional efforts to alter specific clinical problems on measures of dysfunction at home, at school, or in the community are needed before the efficacy of treatment can be decided.

Community-Based Treatments

Background and Underlying Rationale. Unlike other techniques highlighted above, community-based treatments do not include a specific set of techniques. Rather, they refer here to a more general approach toward treatment. The approach challenges basic assumptions about the usual models of treatment and rehabilitation. A basic tenet is that treatment needs to be conducted within the community. Treatment in the community can take advantage of the resources in the everyday environment that can support prosocial behavior. Thus, community-based programs are often conducted in local recreational or youth centers where activity programs are already underway. Integration of treatment in such programs reduces problems of ensuring carry-over of prosocial behavior from treatment to the community settings, a problem likely to arise if the youths are removed from the community (e.g., psychiatric hospital, juvenile correctional facility).

Another tenet is the importance of applying interventions on a relatively large scale. This is in contrast to traditional treatment programs when individuals are identified and selected on a case-by-case basis. The identification, selection, and special treatment raises problems of stigmatization, labeling and crystallization of deviant careers (Feldman et al., 1983; Offord et al., 1986). Treatment needs to be applied in the community where "problem youths" are included along with their prosocial peers. If peer group influences are to be fostered, it is critical that the peers not be other deviant youths. Segregation of deviant youths in residential settings in particular provides them with models for further deviant behavior. Community approaches emphasize the need to integrate and treat antisocial youths and prosocial peers together.

Implicit in the approach is a rejection of a treatment model. Rather than treating selected individuals with problems, the idea is to provide a community intervention that is not under the auspices of mental health, rehabilitation, or legal services. Community programs promote prosocial behavior in large numbers of individuals and work with community services to accomplish their goals. The specific ways in which community-based approaches proceed vary widely. Approaches of other treatments (e.g., individual psychotherapy, behavior therapy) may be utilized as part of the intervention. However, the techniques are integrated with community programs and peer-group influences. Many different community-based interventions have been evaluated, especially for delinquent youths (Lundman, 1984). One recent program for nonadjudicated youths referred for antisocial behavior appears especially promising and is illustrated here.

Feldman and others (1983) conducted a large-scale community-based program that was integrated with activities of the Jewish Community Centers Association in St. Louis. The St. Louis Experiment, as it was called, included youths (ages 8-17) who were referred for antisocial behavior (referred youths) or who normally attended the regular activities programs and were not identified as showing problem behavior (nonreferred youths). The project began with approximately 700 youths; this number declined to approximately 450 by the end of the treatment.

The design of the study was complex because of the interest in evaluating the separate and combined effects of different influences on outcome. The study evaluated the effects of three types of treatment, two levels of therapist experience, and three different ways to compose the groups. The three treatments were *traditional group social work* (focus on group processes, social organization and norms within the group), *behavior modification* (use of reinforcement contingencies, focus on prosocial behavior), and *minimal treatment* (no explicit application of a structured treatment plan; spontaneous interactions of group members). Activity groups within the center were formed and assigned to one of these three interventions. The groups were led by trainers, some of whom were experienced (graduate students of social work with previous experience) and others who were inexperienced (undergraduate students). Finally, the groups were comprised in three ways: all members were youths *referred* for antisocial behavior, all members were *nonreferred* ("normal") youths, and a mixture of *referred and nonreferred.*

The main objective was to evaluate the antisocial behavior of referred youths. Measures were obtained from parents, referral agents, the children, and group leaders as well as direct observations of the groups. The intervention was conducted over a period of a year in which the youths attended sessions and engaged in a broad range of activities (e.g., sports, arts and crafts, fund raising, discussions). The specific treatments were superimposed on the usual activity structure of the community facility. Treatment sessions ranged from 8 to 29 sessions (mean = 22.2 sessions) each lasting about 2-3 hours.

The results indicated that treatment, trainer experience, and group composition exerted impact on at least some of the measures.[4] Youths showed greater reductions in antisocial behavior with experienced rather than inexperienced leaders. Referred (antisocial) youths in mixed groups (that included nonreferred children) showed greater improvements than similar youths in groups comprised of only antisocial youths. Treatments also differed with behavior modification showing greater reductions in antisocial behavior than traditional group treatment. Traditional treatment led to some decrements in behavior relative to the minimal contact group. However, treatment accounted for only a small amount of variance in predicting treatment outcome. For a small subsample (n = 54), follow-up data were available one year later. The follow-up data revealed nonsignificant increases in antisocial behavior based on data from parent and referral agent reports. Yet, the size of the follow-up sample precluded evaluation of the effects of treatment, trainer experience, and group composition.

Overall, the youths in the program benefited, especially in the highly favorable intervention condition (i.e., with an experienced leader, receiving behavior modification, and in a mixed group of referred and nonreferred peers). There remain some ambiguities, as the authors acknowledge. Consider the impact of alternative treatments. Checks on how treatment was carried out revealed a breakdown in treatment integrity. For example, observations of treatment sessions revealed that approximately 35% of the leaders did not implement the behavior modification procedures appropriately for two of the three sessions observed; approximately 44% of the minimal-treatment leaders carried out systematic interventions even though none was supposed to; finally, only 25% of the leaders in the traditional group treatment condition carried out the intervention appropriately. It is difficult to draw conclusions about the relative impact of alternative treatments. It is so rare for studies to even assess treatment integrity that the study should not be faulted on the departures from the intended interventions. Nevertheless, it is still possible that there would be major differences in outcome when the treatments are conducted as intended.

The absence of stronger follow-up data raises other problems. Follow-up was restricted to ratings on nonstandardized measures of antisocial behavior and obtained for a small sample of youths (fewer than 15%). From the data, it is not possible to tell how the vast majority of youths fared. Follow-up data are critical given the possibility that the results might be very different from and even diametrically opposed to the pattern evident immediately after treatment (cf., Jacobson, 1984; Patterson, Levene, & Breger, 1977). Nevertheless, the St. Louis project stands alone in terms of the type of intervention and documentation that has emerged. The project can be closely scrutinized and evaluated because of the type of information that the authors thought to collect and their conceptualization of the analysis. The project demonstrates that change can be achieved in community settings.

Overall Evaluation. The St. Louis project shows that interventions can be delivered on a relatively large scale and can provide benefits for referred (and nonreferred) youths. A community-based approach leaves many questions unanswered. For example, it is not clear that severely antisocial youths as, for example, seen in inpatient and outpatient settings would profit from or even remain in community-based treatments and whether such programs serve better as treatment of disordered children or as preventive efforts for high risk or mildly disturbed children (cf. Offord et al., 1986). Nevertheless, a community approach offers promise and represents a viable alternative for intervention as well as prevention.

General Comments

The above techniques do not exhaust the available options. A multiplicity of techniques such as individual and group psychotherapy, pharmacotherapy, behavior therapy, residential treatment, and others have been applied. Currently, little evidence is available to suggest that these techniques effectively alter antisocial behavior in children and adolescents (see Kazdin, 1985; McCord, 1982; O'Donnell, 1985; Shamsie, 1981). Although the data are sparse for the treatments for antisocial behavior, it would be a mistake to characterize the status of all treatments in the same way.

There are a few generalities that a review of the outcome research supports for particular types of treatment (see Kazdin, 1985). For example, *individual and group therapies* have not been well tested. *Family therapies,* excluding the version highlighted earlier, have rarely been tested in controlled outcome studies where the identified patient is an antisocial child. In contrast, *behavior therapies* have a rather extensive literature showing that various techniques (e.g., reinforcement programs, social skills training) can alter aggressive and other antisocial behaviors. Yet, the focus has tended to be on isolated behaviors rather than a constellation of symptoms. Also, durable changes among clinical samples have been rarely shown, *Pharmacotherapy* has a few recent outcome studies focusing on antisocial youths. Preliminary evidence suggests that lithium and haloperidol can alter aggressive behavior but the effects have not been clearly reflected on measures of behavior in everyday situations, such as, teacher ratings of classroom behavior (Campbell et al., 1984; Platt, Campbell, Green, & Grega, 1984). Conclusions about specific forms of treatment are premature because of somewhat pervasive limitations of the research, noted below.

ISSUES IN CURRENT TREATMENT RESEARCH

Specification of Treatment

Few treatments have been well tested for children and adolescents. Several criteria need to be met. First, the *conceptualization of treatment* is critical. It is important to identify those factors in treatment that address the child's dysfunction and that explain how underlying processes, whether intrapsychic, familial, or social, contribute to antisocial behavior. The conceptualization is important for pointing to the specific treatment components or techniques that will change antisocial behavior and the likely means through which they operate. For example, in parent management training, the conceptualization is based on the view that specific interaction (coercive) patterns lead to escalation of behavior and increase aggressive child behavior. Treatment alters how the parent manages the child to prevent these particular interactions. Here conceptualization of the problem clearly helps to specify exactly what should be done in treatment.

Second, within treatment research it is critical to specify what the procedures are, to the extent possible, and to ensure that the treatment was conducted as intended. If possible, treatments should be delineated in *manual* form that includes written materials to guide the therapist in attaining the specific goals of treatment, and in the procedures, techniques, topics, themes, therapeutic maneuvers, and activities (Luborsky & DeRubeis, 1984). Obviously, some treatments (e.g., behavior therapies) are more easily specified in manual form than others (e.g., interpersonal psychotherapy). With few exceptions, treatments for antisocial behavior are rarely specified in a format that would permit their careful evaluation or training of other therapists.

The specification of treatment is not an end in itself but rather serves a larger purpose. An essential prerequisite of outcome research is to ensure *treatment integrity* (Yeaton & Sechrest, 1981)—that is, that treatment was carried out as intended. Evaluation of treatment integrity requires that some monitoring of the sessions is conducted to ensure that the treatment was actually carried out, that crucial procedures were implemented, and so on. As rudimentary as this sounds, the absence of treatment integrity has plagued outcome research. Conclusions may be reached that a particular technique does not work or that two different techniques show little or no differences in their outcomes when in fact the techniques were not carried out as intended (e.g., Feldman et al., 1983; Jesness, Allison, McCormick, Wedge, & Young, 1975). In general, the absence of clear information about many current treatments for children and adolescents can be traced to the failure to consider the conceptualization of treatment, to specify the procedures, and to evaluate treatment integrity.

Identification of the Clinic Population

Interpretation of current treatment research is obfuscated by the failure to specify crucial information about the children and their families. In many treatment studies, children and adolescents are referred to informally as "emotionally disturbed" or as having "conduct problems." Whether clinical dysfunction is evident is not always clear. In studies when the population evinces clear dysfunction, the failure to use standard diagnostic criteria or widely used assessment devices make it difficult to identify the severity of child dysfunction relative to other samples and to normal (nonreferred) peers.

Interpretation of treatment trials also requires specification of greater details about the parents, family, and home situation. Such variables as single-parent families, parent psychopathology, family size, and marital discord are quite relevant because they are related to long-term prognosis of child behavior and may influence the extent to which treatment can have impact. For example, parent management training does not work with all families. Families with low socioeconomic status, marital discord, greater parental psychopathology, and poor social supports available to the mother show fewer changes with treatment and are not likely to maintain treatment gains (see Kazdin, 1985). This information is critical in making treatment recommendations for the individual clinical case. More generally, identification of the importance of such factors as mediators of therapeutic change has led to incorporation of parental dysfunction into these programs (Griest et al., 1982).

General Comments

Many techniques have been proposed to treat antisocial behavior. Although it is accurate to state that few have been shown to effect therapeutic change, most treatments have not been adequately tested (Sechrest, White, & Brown, 1979). In general, basic methodological standards for developing and evaluating effective therapies (Kazdin, 1986) are more commonly employed in research on the treatment of adults rather than on the treatment of children and adolescents. Consequently, the bulk of the treatment recommendations for children and adolescents stem primarily from anecdotal accounts and descriptions of various approaches and programs rather than firm outcome data (see Schaefer, Briesmeister, & Fitton, 1984).

SUMMARY AND CONCLUSIONS

Many different types of treatment have been applied to antisocial youths. Unfortunately, little outcome evidence exists for most of the techniques. Four types of techniques with the most promising evidence to date were highlighted: parent management training, functional family therapy, problem-solving skills training, and community-based treatment.

Parent management training is directed at altering parent-child interactions in the home, particularly those interactions related to child-rearing practices and coercive interchanges. Research has shown positive outcomes with antisocial children in behavior at home and at school. Moreover the benefits of treatment often are reflected in behaviors of the siblings as well. *Functional family therapy* utilizes principles of systems theory and behavior modification as the basis for altering interactions, communication, and problem solving among family members. Only a few outcome studies are available, but these have consistently shown changes in family process measures and improvements in recidivism among delinquent youths. *Problem-solving skills training* focuses on cognitive processes that underlie social behavior. Few studies have been reported with clinical populations. Yet, the effects of treatment on subclinical levels of dysfunction have been quite promising. *Community-based interventions* usually reflect large-scale programs that are integrated with local services and facilities within the community. One program was reviewed that used a recreational facility and their scheduled activities as a medium for administering alternative interventions.

Significant issues remain to be addressed to accelerate advances in the area of treatment. First, treatments need to be better conceptualized, specified, and monitored while they are implemented. Conclusions about alternative treatments are difficult to draw because of serious conceptual and methodological oversights. Second, careful identification of child, parent, and family characteristics is needed so that the population that receives treatment is clear. Interpretation of many studies is obscured by the paucity of descriptive details about their clinical impairment.

The breadth of dysfunctions of antisocial youths and their families makes the task of developing effective treatments demanding, if not close to impossible. The conceptual connections between current treatment practices and the clinical dysfunctions they can be reasonably expected to alter need to be made explicit. The fact that only a few promising treatments have been identified is not cause for despair. An alternative or rather complementary approach to have impact on the problem is to intervene early, before the full disorder or constellation of symptoms has crystallized. The next chapter focuses on prevention and the efforts to intervene early.

NOTES

1. The number of treatment techniques available for antisocial behavior is vast. Individual techniques and evidence on their behalf have been detailed elsewhere (see Kazdin, 1985).

2. For more in-depth readings on parent management training, the reader is referred to other sources (Dangel & Polster, 1984; Forehand & McMahon, 1981; Patterson, 1982).

3. For additional material on problem-solving skills training, other sources are available (Kendall & Braswell, 1985; Kendall & Hollon, 1979).

4. The results of this study were carefully analyzed and reflect a number of complex interactions that require consultation of the original source (see Feldman et al., 1983).

5

PREVENTION

Based on what is known about antisocial children and their families, treatment is likely to be inherently problematic. Conduct-disordered children are likely to suffer severe and broad-ranging dysfunction. Moreover, untoward family conditions (e.g., marital discord, parent psychopathology) are likely to exacerbate the dysfunction as well as interfere with administration of treatment. Although progress no doubt will be made in identifying effective treatments, prevention is much more attractive on intuitive grounds. Perhaps one can intervene early in the progression of behavior before children have evinced the level of dysfunction characteristic of clinical or adjudicated samples. Moreover, at first blush, implementation of prevention programs may suffer fewer obstacles because the clinical problems of children and their families are not severe or debilitating.

Interest in the prevention of antisocial behavior has been extensive, particularly in relation to delinquency. Reviews have indicated that very few studies have been conducted with adequate research designs and that no effective preventive strategy has been clearly identified (Lundman, 1984; Rutter & Giller, 1983; Sechrest et al., 1979; Wright & Dixon, 1977). Some promising leads are evident in the prevention of antisocial behavior. It is useful to highlight some of the programs to convey current work and the progress that has been made in preventive efforts.

There are, of course, different types of preventive efforts. *Primary prevention* consists of those interventions designed to prevent the development of psychological disorder and to promote the well-being of persons who are as yet unaffected by the dysfunction. Interventions are typically provided widely to unselected groups of persons who do not experience adjustment problems. *Secondary prevention* focuses on those persons who already show some early, mild or moderate signs of dysfunction or are at risk for the clinical problem. Interventions are designed to stop the dysfunction from becoming worse.

The distinction is often blurred in a given study because well-adjusted and high-risk children may be included. For the well-adjusted children, the intervention is clearly directed toward primary prevention; for the high-risk children the intervention is usually directed toward secondary prevention. The programs highlighted here encompass both primary and secondary prevention.[1]

ALTERNATIVE PREVENTION PROGRAMS

Relationship-Based Training Programs

Several prevention programs draw upon models that emphasize the importance of interpersonal relationships, empathy, acceptance, and processes similar to those relied upon in individual psychotherapy. One of the more extensive prevention projects that emphasizes the significance of interpersonal processes is the Primary Mental Health Project (PMHP). The project has been in operation for almost three decades and implemented in over 20 schools in the area of Rochester, New York, where it has been developed. Moreover, the program has been extended to over 300 schools throughout the United States (Cowen, Spinell, Wright, & Weissberg, 1983).

The program is designed to identify high-risk children and to place them in a program to overcome maladjustment. Children identified in primary grades (usually K through 3) as showing "school maladjustment," broadly defined on the basis of teacher ratings of acting out, shyness-anxiety, or learning problems receive the intervention. The intervention consists of establishing a warm accepting relationship with the children, an approach considered to be helpful for all children regardless of their presenting problem (Cowen, Gesten, & Wilson, 1979). Trainers help the children recognize feelings, distinguish between feelings and actions, set limits for inappropriate behavior, and guide children to acceptable ways of behaving. Training is administered individually or occasionally in small groups and encompasses 25 sessions, each averaging 30-40 minutes.

There have been several evaluations of PMHP and its effects over an extended follow-up course. As an illustration, a recent evaluation reported a 2- to 5-year follow-up study of children who completed the program (Chandler, Weissberg, Cowen, & Guare, 1984). The investigation compared children who had been identified at risk and given the program, randomly selected peers matched on demographic variables but who had no adjustment problems, and children with current adjustment problems. Comparison of teacher ratings, self-report measures of social competence, and indices of academic achievement showed that children who received the prevention program fell intermediate in their performance between children with and without adjustment problems. These results suggest that the program improves adjustment, even though the case would be much stronger had students with adjustment problems been assigned randomly to training or no-training conditions and followed over time.

In a comprehensive evaluation of the same program, Weissberg, Cowen, Lotyczewski, and Gesten (1983) reported the outcome effects for seven consecutive annual cohorts of children. Outcome measures included ratings by teachers, aides who administered the program, and their supervisors. The results showed significant improvements in school adjustment. For present purposes, it is important to delineate the results for acting out behaviors, as distinguished from shyness-anxiety and learning problems, the other areas evaluated through teacher ratings. The impact of training was the least evident on acting-out behaviors. Indeed, significant improvements in such behaviors were evident in only 2 of 7 years evaluated. Thus, the effects of the program were at best mixed in relation to antisocial behaviors.

Apart from its widespread dissemination, the PMHP program has spawned additional variations and extensions. In one of these, the program has been adapted for preschool children who are experiencing adjustment problems (Rickel, Dyhdalo, & Smith, 1984; Rickel & Lampi, 1981). High-risk children attending public preschool programs were identified by teacher evaluations of adjustment and assigned to either the intervention or placebo control conditions. In the intervention group, a special program was implemented in which children were encouraged to think and talk of different ways of dealing with problem situations, to play and rehearse social behavior, and to work on child-specific learning difficulties. Control subjects received a supplemental program of traditional activities (e.g., playing with blocks, coloring). The intervention was administered individually at school four times per week for 8 months for each child. Parents of experimental subjects also received sessions to focus on their child-rearing practices to help promote prosocial behavior. Control parents participated in nondirective discussions related to their parenting experiences.

Experimental subjects showed greater improvements in adjustment and teacher ratings than control subjects. Two years after the program, the gains were still evident. Moreover, treated subjects were no different from a low-risk (well-adjusted) group of children. For present purposes, it is important to note that initially shy and withdrawn children showed greater gains over the course of follow-up than aggressive children. This finding is consistent with those of the PMHP program where aggressive children have fared less well.

Among relationship-based interventions, the PMHP stands out as exemplary. Such excellent features have included programmatic development and evaluation, successful implementation and dissemination in the schools, and the development of an extensive training program for paraprofessionals who administer the procedures. Also, follow-up assessment over a period of years after students complete the program is rare in the treatment or prevention literatures in general.

There are limitations that have been recognized as well such as the heavy reliance upon quasi-experimental designs rather than controlled trials with random assignment, the use of measures completed by persons who are actively involved in the program or who are aware of student participation, and the relatively small improvements (effect sizes) associated with the intervention (Stein & Polyson, 1984). The focus on school maladjustment in general, the application of a single intervention to prevent an omnibus set of problems, and the absence of clear data on the extent to which children who have been screened genuinely are at risk for future psychiatric impairment are questions that remain to be addressed. The program has shown that school performance and measures of adjustment can be altered. For present purposes, strong evidence is not available to indicate that conduct disorder can be averted.

Cognitively Based Interventions

A large number of prevention programs have utilized cognitively based approaches including problem-solving skills training, as discussed in the previous chapter.[2] For example, Shure and Spivack (1982) evaluated the impact of their problem-solving skills training program with black, inner-city children (ages 4-5), many of whom presumably would be at risk for behavior problems. The program was implemented by teachers and evaluated over a 2-year period. No-treatment control children were also included. The immediate impact of training was evident on problem-solving skills and classroom adjustment. Interestingly, at a 2-year follow-up assessment, adjusted youths who had participated in the program were less likely to show behavioral problems than similar youths who had not received the program. Overall, the study showed the impact of problem-solving skills training on youths with and without adjustment problems. The reduced likelihood of behavioral problems has obvious preventive implications. On the other hand, youths were not specifically identified as at risk for serious antisocial behaviors; extrapolation of program effects to youths at risk for such behaviors is premature.

In a different cognitively based procedure, Block (1978) evaluated the effects of rational-emotive training with male and female high school students (mean age = 16 years). The students were selected because of a history of disruptive behavior, poor grades, high rate of absences and tardiness, and cutting classes. Youths were assigned randomly to rational-emotive training, human-relations training, or no treatment. Rational-emotive training focused on self-examination and self-questioning, confrontation, and various conceptually related themes. Human-relations training focused on discussions of psychodynamic topics. Both treatment groups met 5 days per week (45 min per session) for a 12-week period. Evaluations near the end of treatment and a 4-month follow-up after treatment revealed that rational-emotive training showed significantly greater increases than the other treatment and control conditions in grade-point average, decreases in disruptive behavior, and cutting of classes. Youths in the human-relations condition did not systematically improve on these measures. The results also are significant in that they show the impact of school-based interventions with high-risk youths.

Cognitively based programs have been implemented in the schools as part of a curriculum designed to prevent maladjustment. In a programmatic set of studies, Gesten, Weissberg and their colleagues have introduced problem-solving skills training in second through fourth grades. The program trains children in class to develop a problem-solving approach to interpersonal problems and to apply the approach to real-life situations (e.g., Gesten et al., 1982; Weissberg & Gesten, 1982; Weissberg et al., 1981). The program has evolved over the last several years and has varied in duration. More recent versions have included approximately 40 to 50 lessons in class administered over a 4-month period. The results have shown clear changes in problem-solving skills, although changes in ratings of adjustment and classroom behaviors have been less evident. Some gains in adjustment appear to be sustained at least up to a 1-year follow-up relative to controls who have not received training (Gesten et al., 1982).

The above and other problem-solving skills approaches to prevention have produced promising results at different elementary grade levels (e.g., see Kendall & Hollon, 1979). As with many of the cognitively based treatment studies, the results for prevention studies have shown that changes are relatively consistent on various measures of cognitive processes and problem-solving skills and modest, tentative, and often nonexistent on measures of adjustment. Measures of antisocial behavior might be even less likely to show improvements than measures of the more general characteristic of adjustment, because the latter characteristic includes a variety of internalizing symptoms, social behaviors, and mild behavior problems possibly less recalcitrant to change. Thus, cognitively based preventive strategies have yet to show impact on the primary behaviors of interest here.

Behavioral Interventions

Several studies have evaluated various behavioral techniques with high risk youths. Durlak (1980) compared the effects of behavioral and relationship programs conducted in the schools with no treatment. High-risk youths in grades 1 through 3 were identified through teacher ratings of school maladjustment. Youths were then randomly assigned to one of the three conditions. The behavioral program consisted of providing token and social reinforcement to children for performing prosocial classroom behaviors. Relationship therapy consisted of nondirective treatment and emphasized a warm, trusting, and empathic relationship. After 10 weeks of treatment, youths judged to be improved were terminated; others continued for another 10-week period.

In general, the results favored the behavioral treatment. More children were improved by this intervention and within a shorter period than with relationship therapy. On ratings of acting-out behaviors, behavioral and relationship conditions did not differ, although as already noted more youths in the behavioral condition were terminated early because of their gains. Analyses suggested that youths who were more maladjusted at the beginning of treatment and who continued for extended training improved but still evinced significant levels of maladjustment at the end of training. The results suggest the potential of behavioral approach for less severely maladjusted youths. The findings need to be qualified given the awareness of teachers of experimental and control conditions to which children were assigned and the reliance upon teacher ratings alone, points acknowledged by the author.

A behavioral program conducted in the public schools for so-called troublesome adolescents was reported by Wodarski and his colleagues (1979). Seventh- and eighth-grade students with academic and social problems were assigned to experimental or no-treatment conditions. Experimental subjects received academic training, social skills training, and family skills training involving parents in home management techniques and involvement in school activities. Posttreatment comparisons showed improvements on several measures of academic and social skills performance. Follow-up 1 year later showed fewer suspensions and disciplinary referrals in the school and higher school attendance and grade point averages among experimental youths. However, a 4-year follow-up indicated very few differences among social and problem behaviors (on 10 of 119 measures). The most reasonable conclusion is that the program was not effective in the long run.

In another project, reinforcement procedures were implemented in a large-scale community program for youths (ages 11 to 17) referred from a number of agencies for their behavioral and academic problems (Fo & O'Donnell, 1975; O'Donnell, Lygate, & Fo, 1979). Some of the youths who participated had prior arrest records; others did not. Hence, as the authors suggest, the project at once addressed treatment (remediation of adjudicated youths) and prevention (for those at risk for delinquency). Individual behavior modification programs using contingency contracts for child-specific problem behaviors constituted the program.

Youths with prior arrest records profited from the program in showing reduced arrest records compared to control subjects who did not receive treatment. In contrast, youths without prior arrest records showed *greater* arrest records than controls. Evaluation 2 years later showed these effects were sustained. Thus, the program was effective in remediation but counterproductive in prevention. Stated more plainly, the program clearly made some children worse.

In another community-based behavioral program designed to prevent delinquency, operant conditioning techniques were used (Davidson & Wolfred, 1977). While in effect, the program altered academic and social behaviors. However, follow-up assessment 3 and 9 months after completion of the program failed to reveal differences favoring experimental subjects over no-treatment controls. In fact, experimental youths appeared to become worse in terms of contacts with the justice system and subsequent institutionalization.

The above studies convey the mixed results of behavioral prevention programs conducted in different settings and varying in focus. The effects have been clearest on measures obtained while the program is in effect. Continued effects after the program has been terminated are less clear. In a few programs, some youths have become worse following treatment.

Community Work and Activities Programs

Prevention programs occasionally have involved at risk youths in work or activity programs in the community. The rationale in general is to involve youths in prosocial activities, to teach new skills, and to build peer group connections in the context of these skill domains. The specific tasks or skill areas are also considered to be important in improving self-esteem and a sense of competence and in providing a source of activity for idle time that otherwise might be devoted to antisocial behavior. Two programs illustrate community approaches to prevention.

Hackler and Hagan (1975) conducted a prevention program in communities with high official delinquency rates. Youths (ages 14 to 15) were recruited and randomly assigned to alternative experimental and control groups. Experimental subjects participated in work groups where they performed community work (e.g., in parks, housing projects) one day a week for over a year and/or spent one afternoon per week learning tasks with the aid of teaching machines. The latter experience was designed to provide a sense of competence and success rather than remedial education. Control subjects received neither of the above experiences.

Follow-up 3 years after the program had been terminated revealed that youths who had participated in work groups became worse than controls as measured by police contacts. In contrast, youths who had worked on teaching machines showed a reduced rate of police contact in comparison to controls. There were some interactions of treatment with subject characteristics. White children seemed to show reduced police contact after the work experience, whereas black children showed increased contact. Also, disadvantaged youths, as defined by lower IQ and referred to the project because of problem behavior, tended to profit less well from the program. Overall, the surprising finding is the deleterious effects generally associated with the work experience.

Offord and his colleagues (1986; Offord & Jones, 1983) reported an extensive community-based program in a housing project in Canada with over 400 children (ages 5-15) from poverty-level families. The youths were considered to be at high risk for antisocial behavior. Some of the youths already had contact with police for their behavioral problem. The project was designed to involve youths in activity programs in the community and to train specific skills in several areas (e.g., swimming, hockey, dancing, and musical instruments). The effects of training in skill areas and the increased involvement in activities in the community, the investigators posited, would spill over to reductions in antisocial behavior in the community and school performance.

In a quasi-experimental design, two housing projects were selected. One project received the experimental intervention; the other did not. The specific skill development program for the children, the core intervention, was a highly systematic program based on the child's initial skill level. Careful assessment was conducted to evaluate child progress and rewards were provided for attendance and participation. The skill-training intervention programs were implemented over a period of 32 months and evaluated on diverse measures.

The results revealed no significant differences between experimental and control (nonintervention) youths on parent and teacher evaluations of deviant behavior. However, significant differences were evident on community measures including the number of police charges against the youths, calls to the fire department, and security violations in the community (e.g., broken windows). In each case, the experimental community showed lower rates of the behaviors. Yet for the youths, the overall rate of offenses did not change; the changes in the number of instances in which official charges for crimes were made by police but no difference in the number of offenses were interpreted as a reduction in the severity of offenses in the experimental group. A follow-up assessment conducted 16 months after treatment had been terminated indicated that offenses and security violations increased. However, the level did not approach the preintervention rates.

Other Approaches

Community programs illustrated above have a specific focus (e.g., skill activities) but may include other ingredients within the community. Contact with parents and community agencies and assistance in specific areas (e.g., transportation) are provided often to facilitate implementation of the treatment or to enhance acceptability of the program to the community more generally. Yet, high-risk communities have broad needs for programs and it is reasonable to implement intensive programs to address multiple needs that may impact on the families and their ability to cope. Occasionally, broad-based and intensive intervention programs are provided to prevent childhood problems.

As one example, Johnson and Breckenridge (1982) conducted a parent-child education program for children ages 1-3 years old. The program was designed to prevent behavioral problems in young children and was offered to low-income Mexican American families. Families were assigned to the two-year intervention program or no treatment. The program addressed a variety of parent and child issues including parent-child interaction to foster cognitive development; provided assistance to the parents in learning English, and utilizing community resources; focused on practical issues related to health, safety, and child care; and provided instruction, practice, and feedback in developing child-management techniques, to mention major components. The program totaled approximately 500 hours of participation and involved all family members at different points.

Follow-up assessment 1 to 4 years after the program revealed decreases in destructive behavior and overactivity for intervention rather than for control children, as evident on selected measures from parent interviews. These results were restricted to boys rather than girls. As the authors note, neither control nor intervention youths showed serious behavioral problems.

The intensity of the effort required to achieve impact was addressed in a school-based program where the intervention was provided over a 2-year period (Bien & Bry, 1980; Bry, 1982; Bry & George, 1980). Sixth- and seventh-grade youths selected because of their discipline problems and low academic motivation were assigned randomly to one of three interventions or a no intervention control condition. The interventions provided increasingly more intensive efforts to alter student behavior. With the first condition, teacher conferences were scheduled by program staff to focus attention and programs on individual children with problems. In the second condition, teacher conferences were held but group meetings with the children were also scheduled and special programs were devised to help the children with school activities. The programs for the children included reinforcement for classroom behavior and school performance (e.g., attendance) and practice in appropriate classroom behavior. In the third condition, teacher conferences and group meetings with the children were scheduled but parent conferences were also held.

Essentially, the group with all three ingredients, involving contact with teachers, students, and parents was the only condition preventing further deterioration in grades. Interventions without all three ingredients were no better than the no intervention group. At follow-up assessment 1 and 5 years later, intervention youths evinced greater employment, less drug abuse, less reported criminal behavior, and fewer school problems than controls. Up to 5 years after treatment, intervention subjects showed fewer court contacts than control youths.

Overall Evaluation

Several of the programs noted above have gone beyond merely showing promising results. In a number of demonstrations, adjustment and social competence have been altered by early intervention. The efforts have been directed primarily at lowering the incidence of psychiatric or behavioral disorders among youths who are at risk, as well as developing social competencies and improving adaptation.

The broad goals of many prevention programs make their impact somewhat difficult to evaluate in the context of the present topic. Although the outcomes occasionally have been impressive, the extent to which any of the programs prevents serious psychiatric dysfunction or antisocial behavior is not clear. If anything, the results from some of the programs have suggested that antisocial behavior is less likely to be altered than other types of dysfunction and that overt behaviors, when assessed, may be less likely to reflect change than global ratings of adjustment. There are conspicuous exceptions where the impact in fact is evaluated on antisocial behavior in the community (Offord et al., 1986). In general, the data available at this time do not seem to support implementation of any large-scale prevention program to alter antisocial behavior.

Efforts to evaluate prevention programs with specific reference to antisocial behavior need to be increased. The above studies demonstrate that programs can be reasonably disseminated as part of classroom curricula or a community-based program. What is needed to make the efforts clearly relevant to the present topic is more systematic evaluation of psychiatric impairment, incidence of conduct disorder, and performance of antisocial behaviors in the community as part of outcome assessment.

MAJOR ISSUES AND OBSTACLES

The objectives of prevention are relatively straightforward—intervene early and controvert the course leading to antisocial behavior. The range of obstacles readily explains the little progress that can be documented to date.

Early Identification of Youths At Risk

Obviously, a critical point of departure for preventive efforts is identifying children at risk.[3] This task would seem to be not that difficult because the risk-factor research reviewed earlier was relatively clear in noting the child, parent, family, and other (e.g., school) factors that relate to the onset of antisocial behavior. Among the factors, those features related to the child's own behavior (early signs of antisocial behavior and unmanageability) were generally the best predictors of later dysfunction.

There are two related obstacles in early identification. The first pertains to some of the limits of identification of children on the basis of their early childhood behavior. Both longitudinal and cross-sectional studies have shown that disruptive, problematic, and antisocial behavior have a relatively high prevalence rate in early childhood. These behaviors can be seen early in adjusted children whose long-term course is not likely to include antisocial behavior. Among so-called *normal* low-risk children, there is a tendency for such behaviors to decline over the course of development. Yet, efforts to select high-risk children could inadvertently yield a large number of cases for whom such behaviors do not portend subsequent dysfunction.

The related problem is the difficulty in predicting accurately who among those children at risk will show problematic behavior. Different sorts of variables and algorithms have been evaluated in an effort to predict who will become delinquent. For example, in one of the more well-controlled studies, Farrington (1975) compared alternative methods of combining child, parent, and family variables to predict who would become delinquent. The study represented a longitudinal investigation identifying children at approximately age 8 and following them through early adulthood. The results indicated that even with the best combination of predictors, only approximately 50% of the delinquent youths could be correctly identified. Essentially the problem for prevention work is the less than ideal rates for identification of *true positives* (i.e., persons who are high on the risk factors early in life and who eventually show the problem). Obviously related are the corresponding measures that reflect the problems of selection, namely, the presence of *false positives* (i.e., persons who are high on the risk factors and identified as likely to show the problem but who do not), and the presence of *false negatives* (i.e., persons who do not appear to be at risk but who eventually show the problem).

At this point, the ability to predict who will show clinically severe antisocial behavior is weak (cf. Loeber & Dishion, 1983). The enterprise of making such predictions is quite complex, to say the least. The specific factors that serve as the best set of predictors vary as a function of the age that the child is evaluated whether in early or middle childhood and the criteria that are predicted such as police or court contacts, conviction, or self-reported delinquent acts (see Farrington, 1975; Loeber & Dishion, 1983). Under the best circumstances, identification of high-risk children based on the many sets of variables that relate to onset of dysfunction is also likely to select significant proportions of persons who will never show the problem (false positives) and to miss others who will (false negatives).

Given the above, there is at the outset a weakness in the enterprise of preventing antisocial behavior. Perhaps a significant proportion of high-risk youths will manifest disturbance in adolescence and adulthood. However, there is another proportion that will not. Moreover, many youths who are not at risk at the time a preventive effort begins and who do not receive the intervention may evince problems later (Wenar, 1984). The fact that children grow out of as well as into problems reduces the efficiency and efficacy of preventive efforts in ameliorating a particular problem.

The model of prevention often includes the application of interventions on a large-scale rather than for individual children. Thus, if antisocial behavior cannot be predicted as well as one would like, perhaps it would be just as well to utilize the risk factors but not to be restrictive in selecting children and adolescents for intervention programs. Thus, one might loosen the selection criteria with the idea of obtaining those at high risk as well as many others. Stated differently, the selection criteria can be lenient so as to minimize false negatives (youths who do not seem at risk but in fact are) at the risk of inadvertently obtaining a few more false positives (youths who are not at risk but seem to be on the selection criteria). Such a strategy would be quite defensible, if not wise, were it not for the possibility that those false positives could be adversely influenced by the program.

First Do No Harm

A related issue is the potential effects of preventive efforts other than those that are intended. There has been an assumption that if preventive efforts prove ineffective, at least they will not harm. However, this can be questioned. Prevention or treatment efforts are not necessarily either beneficial or neutral. Efforts to prevent antisocial behavior can produce deleterious effects.

Certainly the best-known example is the Cambridge-Somerville Youth Study, which was designed to prevent delinquency (Powers & Witmer, 1951). The study involved over 500 boys including those at risk for delinquency. Children received either a broad-based and not too well-specified treatment (involving psychiatric and medical attention, academic assistance, repeated contact with a counselor, and community programs) or no treatment. Follow-up 30 years after treatment (McCord, 1978) revealed that those who were in the treated group showed a higher rate of criminal activity, alcoholism, serious disease, symptoms of stress, lower job status and satisfaction, and death at an earlier age. The adverse effects have drawn attention to the possibility that intervening may be harmful.

More recent evidence (e.g., Fo & O'Donnell, 1975; Hackler & Hagan, 1975), as noted earlier, has corroborated the risk of deleterious effects with preventive interventions. The occasional deleterious effects should not be used to discourage preventive efforts. Indeed, such efforts are in dire need given the incidence of antisocial behavior and the absence of clearly effective treatments. Yet, there is a problem with the application of prevention strategies en masse. Those who are not genuinely at risk for antisocial behavior *before* the program may well be at increased risk *after* their participation. In most cases, it is hoped, the outcomes of prevention programs are either positive or benign. However, the risk for deleterious effects can no longer be considered a remote possibility.

Conducting Research on Prevention

There are a number of obstacles that may make prevention research unusually difficult. At the outset, the initial task of any prevention research project usually is to make the case that an intervention is needed. A perennial problem for psychological or medical prevention programs is to convey to potential participants that an intervention is needed in the absence of a felt clinical problem (Glidewell, 1983). The absence of symptoms is perceived as no problem, making the need for an intervention unpersuasive to would-be participants. Establishing the need for the intervention requires firmly convincing people of the connection between a risk factor and the ultimate problem. The case has been heavily promoted for some problems (e.g., drawing the connection to the public between hypertension—the silent killer—and risk of a heart attack). It may be more difficult to establish the case as readily for psychological, psychiatric, and behavorial problems.

Once the case is made convincingly that the intervention is needed, it is difficult to convey the need among participants for a no-treatment control condition. Prevention research is invariably longitudinal so that a true test of the intervention comes from comparing the treated group with the untreated group to see in the next several years whether the antisocial behaviors, clinical referrals, delinquency rates, and other measures of interest are reduced. The no-treatment group is usually needed to address the base rates of change over the course of development. Yet, it is unclear why participants would remain in such a group if they believed that their children were truly at risk and in need of a program of some sort.

Another obstacle is the seemingly undramatic outcomes that successful prevention programs promise (Glidewell, 1983). If successful, the intervention will lead to the absence of specific problems or generally improved adjustment. One could argue that for a particular child, the problem might not have emerged anyway. Thus, the effect of the intervention is not obvious. In contrast, treatment in any given case may yield a dramatic effect, as evident in a total remission of symptoms. The before and after differences in the behavior of a successfully treated case are highly persuasive and make the case for and potential benefits of treatment obvious; the analogue of a successful prevention program is a "before and before" description where the problem was not there to begin with and never was evident later.

There are other related issues as well. Identification of children for a prevention project can inadvertently label them as problematic or at risk. Given the prediction data, many of these children might not eventually show any antisocial behavior. Their early labeling as at risk introduces the potential for stigma, if not a self-fulfilling prophesy, based on reactions of teachers and peers. In the case of a *treatment study* such labeling may also occur but by that time there is an identified clinical problem. Presumably to the parent, the importance of the problem outweighs the concern of any risks associated with labeling. The case may be different for a prevention study. Indeed, the concern for labeling and stigmatizing youths and their families has served as one of the reasons for community-wide interventions (Feldman et al., 1983; Offord et al., 1986).

General Comments

In the chapter on treatment, many obstacles and difficulties were identified that have impeded high quality research. The tasks for conducting prevention research are often much more difficult. Many of the prevention studies highlighted earlier have utilized paraprofessionals as trainers, have conducted multifaceted programs across multiple settings (home and community) in a single investigation, and have administered assessments repeatedly over protracted periods. Obstacles associated with training therapists, maintaining integrity of treatment, and coordinating the interventions across settings are particularly acute for prevention studies. Given these difficulties, the quality of prevention research, by and large, has been rather admirable. There still remain very basic questions, such as whether any intervention designed to prevent conduct disorder can actually do so. Yet, this too may be an unnecessarily stringent criterion, especially at present, when any modest sign of progress in a well-controlled intervention study would be a major finding. At this point, it would be valuable to have demonstrations showing that reliable reductions could be achieved in the incidence of conduct disorder or the severity of dysfunction over the long-term among high-risk youths.

SUMMARY AND CONCLUSIONS

There have been many prevention programs, particularly for children identified as at risk for later maladjustment. Several of these programs have shown positive changes in child functioning years after the intervention has been terminated. An interesting feature is that the interventions often have been implemented in the schools and communities and on a relatively large scale. Thus, the technology for delivering many different interventions and for their evaluation is well established.

A difficulty that pervades the literature is the somewhat generic goals of prevention programs, namely to decrease risk for dysfunction and to improve well-being and adjustment. These goals are laudatory and significant to be sure. However, in the case of a specific interest, as with the present task at hand, conclusions about antisocial behavior are difficult to draw. As in the case of treatment, there are many promising prevention strategies. Few evaluations provide specific reference to the prevention of antisocial behavior, conduct disorder, and delinquency.

Prevention of antisocial behavior is a goal that continues to hold great hope. There are however major obstacles inherent in the enterprise that make difficult the identification and implementation of effective programs. Identification and recruitment of high-risk children or families raise special problems. The problems are not insurmountable. The scope of the effort that is needed has already been evident in selected studies where the primary limitation has been the failure to focus on and measure antisocial behavior rather than more global measures of adjustment.

NOTES

1. For reviews of different types of prevention programs, the reader is referred elsewhere (Roberts & Peterson, 1984; Winett, Stefanek, & Riley, 1983).
2. Many of the treatment studies reviewed earlier focus on children with mild adjustment problems. As such, the research can be viewed as treatment outcome because the goal is direct reduction of maladaptive behavior or as secondary prevention with the object of delimiting the severity and course of the problem. The studies illustrated here focus on identifying adjusted or high risk cases.
3. We will discuss here the case of identifying children at risk for the prevention of later antisocial behavior, say, in adolescence. The case might be addressed differently such as identifying adolescents who are at risk and preventing adult antisocial behavior.

6

New Directions And Models For Research

The previous chapters have highlighted research in several areas related to antisocial behavior in children and adolescents. With such a broad-based research effort, involving multiple disciplines, progress is likely to be made in understanding conduct disorder and in developing effective treatments. Yet, it is important to identify models, views, and approaches that underlie current research, to study their limitations, and to suggest different models that might offer fresh approaches. The present chapter discusses the need to consider different models from those in current use in two central areas of work—namely, the delineation and treatment of antisocial behavior.

DELINEATION AND DIAGNOSIS OF ANTISOCIAL BEHAVIOR

Progress has been made with both clinically derived and multivariate diagnoses in elaborating the constellation of antisocial behaviors. Work on both fronts continues to progress, as reflected in ongoing revisions of alternative diagnostic systems (e.g., DSM-III, the International Classification of Diseases). Research on diagnosis continues primarily at the level of larger constellations of behaviors. The clinical picture, family correlates, clinical course, response to treatment, and similar factors are studied to identify and define a disorder. As for the study of subtypes, there has been consistent recognition of aggressive and socialized delinquent youths. Other subtypes (discussed in Chapter 2) are much less universally recognized. Although future work on delineating antisocial behavior no doubt will continue to progress, different lines of work might accelerate advances in the diagnosis of conduct disorder. Two such directions are the increased specificity in identifying symptom patterns and expansion of the dimensions that are considered in diagnosis.

Increased Specificity

Current diagnosis focuses on Conduct Disorder, a rather heterogeneous class of antisocial and obstreporous behaviors. There is little question that a broad diagnosis can be reliably and meaningfully made. Yet, different arguments lobby for greater specificity for understanding antisocial behavior. First, examining global classes of heterogeneous children and adolescents may mask identification of subtypes and effective strategies for their management and treatment. For example, youths may differ widely in chronicity, age, and patterns of dysfunction. Interventions appropriate for selected subsamples may not show overall effects when applied to the heterogeneous class, "conduct disorder."

Second, scrutiny of subpopulations of antisocial youths reveals major definitional problems in the identification of cases and assessment of dysfunction. The difficulties in identifying cases are often glossed over and the implications are ignored when a general, heterogeneous group of conduct disorder children is sought. The difficulties are readily apparent when efforts are made to study a particular subpopulation.

For example, *truancy* or persistent absence from school is one of the symptoms of conduct disorder. Identification of truancy would seem to be straightforward, because children can be selected from school records and parents can be asked about the reasons for child absenteeism. Moreover, because school attendance is compulsory, detection should be facilitated. Yet, identifying index cases for study is difficult because the problems in distinguishing excused from unexcused absences, in delineating unexcused absences unbeknownst to the parent from absences due to school phobia and school refusal, and in overcoming biases of clinicians in assigning the label "truant" to children because of the legal implications for the parents such as fines and loss of custody (see Galloway, 1985). The definitional issues are not academic but are at the core of understanding the clinical problem, its prevalence, characteristics, and likely points of effective intervention. The problems of defining truancy and identifying index cases derive from an intensive study of the problem rather than larger grouping of individuals in the heterogeneous class of Conduct Disorder.

As another example, *firesetting* is a symptom of conduct disorder and one that also should be easily identified because of the discrete nature of the behavior. Here too basic problems emerge at the definitional level that have critical implications for understanding the problem. What defines a firesetter? Playing with matches, lighting small fires of no consequence, or arson involving major damage or injury are among many alternatives. Often firesetting relies upon reports of the child or parent. Child and parent may disagree on the occurrence of firesetting, unless a specific act was known to the family perhaps because it occurred in the home (e.g., setting fire to one's room). However, much of the firesetting may be outside the home. The child may be the only one in the family who knows of an incident and may simply not report it.

The ambiguities of defining truancy and firesetting raise important methodological problems that require new assessment tools and clearer criteria to operationalize the dysfunction. These procedures in turn draw attention to the different levels of severity and different manifestations of the behavior. The ultimate end is a finer-grained analysis of the problem.

An advantage to seeking increased specificity in the focus on behavioral problems is to permit the development of mini-theories about a problem area. A mini-theory accounts for specific facets of conduct disorder rather than attempt a comprehensive explanation of how the full range of dysfunctions has emerged. For example, Patterson (1982) has developed coercion theory to explain the development of aggressive behavior in the homes of antisocial youths. The theory might be criticized for the many questions left unanswered (e.g., why a particular child rather than a sibling becomes aggressive) or for neglecting to incorporate important influences on aggressive behavior (e.g., genetic contributions, TV violence). Yet, such criticism fails to acknowledge the remarkable research that this model has spawned. The limited focus of the theory has aided rather than hindered conceptualization of the entire range of antisocial behaviors by uncovering subgroups (e.g., aggressors, stealers) for whom specific processes are less applicable. Although not as well developed or tested, mini-theories have emerged to explain truancy (Galloway, 1985) and firesetting (Kolko & Kazdin, 1986). Such efforts raise hopes for finer-grained analyses of these subgroups of antisocial children.

Although advances in diagnosis continue to emerge seeking to understand conduct disorder and antisocial behavior at a more general level, research on more focused problem areas is essential as well. The increased need for specificity in studying antisocial behavior does not compete with the goals of diagnosis. Indeed, studying more specific behavioral patterns has the overall goal of identifying better ways of organizing or grouping the phenomena for theoretical and clinical purposes.

Expansion of Focus

The above discussion argues for greater specificity in studying antisocial youths than current diagnostic concepts promote. There is also a need for diagnosis to expand along different dimensions. Currently, the explicit orientation of clinical diagnosis is on the *problem of the child.* Yet, an analysis at the level of the individual is incomplete. Antisocial behavior is not merely a problem of the individual child or adolescent. Rather, the behavior must be viewed in the context of alternative systems, particularly that of the family. The empirical literature repeatedly points to the family as a training ground for antisocial behavior and as a predictor of long-term course. To provide an account of conduct disorder and to make predictions about clinical course may require elaborating and meaningfully classifying important family factors.

There are no doubt complex classification systems that could be applied to families of antisocial children. An obstacle to making advances would be to find a conceptually neutral descriptive system that a quorum of professionals would accept. Yet, a relatively neutral system to classify families could be based on such dimensions as parental psychopathology and marital dysfunction, history of antisocial behavior, social disadvantage, and perhaps other areas that have empirical support as relevant to antisocial youths and their problems.

Operationally, these areas can be measured with many available assessment tools.

To make progress initially, a complex system utilizing information on diverse variables to diagnose families is not needed. Consider, by way of analogy, research on the impact of child temperament on subsequent adjustment. Many different patterns of temperament have been identified along with a host of characteristics upon which children can be graded (Thomas & Chess, 1977). Yet, there has been value in developing a general system incorporating multiple dimensions and grouping children as "easy to difficult" in terms of their early childhood temperament. No one doubts that this single continuum oversimplifies the complexity and richness of individual differences. However, the empirical findings showing predictable differences with this simple classification system establish its heuristic value (see Plomin, 1983). Gross classification systems (e.g., children vs. adults) are frequently helpful, although there is widespread recognition that they fail to make important distinctions within a group.

Perhaps as an initial point of departure, families could be classified along the lines that evaluated alternative risk factors. The specific factors that could be used and the algorithm for combining them can draw from research attempting to identify predictors of antisocial behavior and continuation of this behavior once it has emerged (e.g., Farrington, 1978). A tally of those factors for which a given family is *positive*—that is, in the direction of risk—could be made and presumably high and low risk families could be identified. The adaptation of risk factor research here is to develop a way to distinguish families of antisocial youths and to identify relevant dimensions that predict clinical course, response to treatment, and long-term adjustment.

In general, an important direction for diagnosis of antisocial child behavior would be to expand upon the focus and models. The present comments suggest that the family be examined first, given research on the impact of this system on antisocial children and adolescents. The focus on other areas (e.g., peer relations and bonding) could be argued as well. The family was mentioned to convey the need to expand the model of diagnosis of conduct disorder rather than to imply that only one domain is relevant. Ideally, a classification system could be developed to evaluate multiple domains of functioning (e.g., at home, at school; social behavior, academic competence). The result would be a profile of antisocial youths and the environments from which they emerged.[1]

INTERVENTION RESEARCH

Current Prospects

Throughout previous chapters two consistent themes have been the seriousness of the problem of antisocial behavior and the absence of treatments with demonstrated efficacy. These messages are important to convey to help mobilize the level of social concern and scientific effort needed for progress. There is an important other side that is equally critical. In the present context, the focus has been primarily on the level of severity of antisocial behavior that is diagnosable clinically as conduct disorder. However, antisocial behavior can be viewed on a continuum of severity with points that are delineated as those of clinical or social significance. The broader question of interest is the extent to which treatments are currently available for antisocial behavior across the full spectrum of severity.

Consider for a moment all children and adolescents who, with a broad definition, might be considered to evince antisocial behavior. Consider further that this population can be represented by different levels of severity as reflected in oversimplistic terms such as *mild, moderate,* and *extreme.*[2] "Mild" refers to those children who are oppositional, obstreperous, and bothersome to parents and teachers. For present purposes, let us view these children as more than occasionally bothersome or obnoxious but clearly subclinical in severity of their behavior. At the other end of the continuum is "extreme" antisocial behavior; this level refers to severely disturbed children, clinically diagnosable and/or adjudicated youths. Obviously, the three levels are arbitrary and reflect a continuum.

It is likely that the prevalence of antisocial behavior is in part a function of the level of severity that is to define the behaviors with many more mild than extreme children and adolescents. For purposes of discussion, Figure 6.1 provides a hypothetical representation of the three levels of antisocial behavior with hypothetical proportions of their relative frequency. For the three groups that are represented, conclusions about *currently available* treatments may differ greatly. Children in the extreme group evince the more severe levels of deviance (e.g., most chronic cases, broad range of antisocial behaviors) and the highest level of personal and family risk factors. Currently,

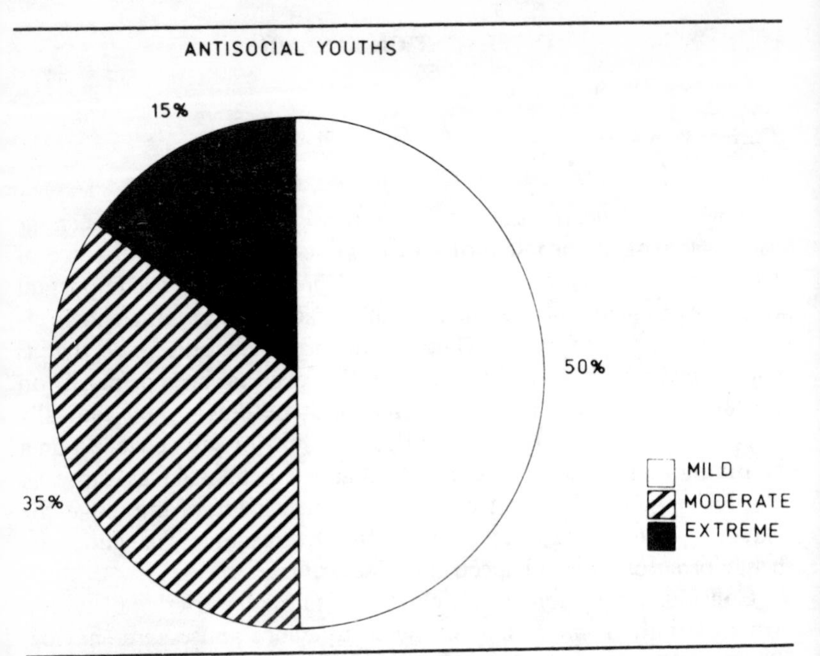

Figure 6.1 **Hypothetical illustration of approximate proportions of youths who might be regarded as showing mild, moderate, or extreme levels of antisocial behavior.**

research has little to recommend for this group, although there are promising treatments, as noted before.

If we turn to mild levels of the problem, the prospects for effective treatment among currently available options is rather good. For mild and many moderate levels of severity, a large proportion of children and families probably can be effectively treated. Stated more generally, it is likely that the effectiveness of treatment varies inversely with the severity of the problem. Thus, for all children who might be classified as showing mild, moderate, and extreme antisocial behavior, one might find the proportion who can be effectively treated to look something like the hypothetical function in Figure 6.2. Again, it is critical to keep in mind that the general relation is being advanced here rather than the classification system (mild, moderate, extreme) or proportions of persons who could be effectively treated.

Although the specifics are hypothetical, data are already available showing the effectiveness of treating mild versions of antisocial behavior. For example, one effective program involves *brief parent*

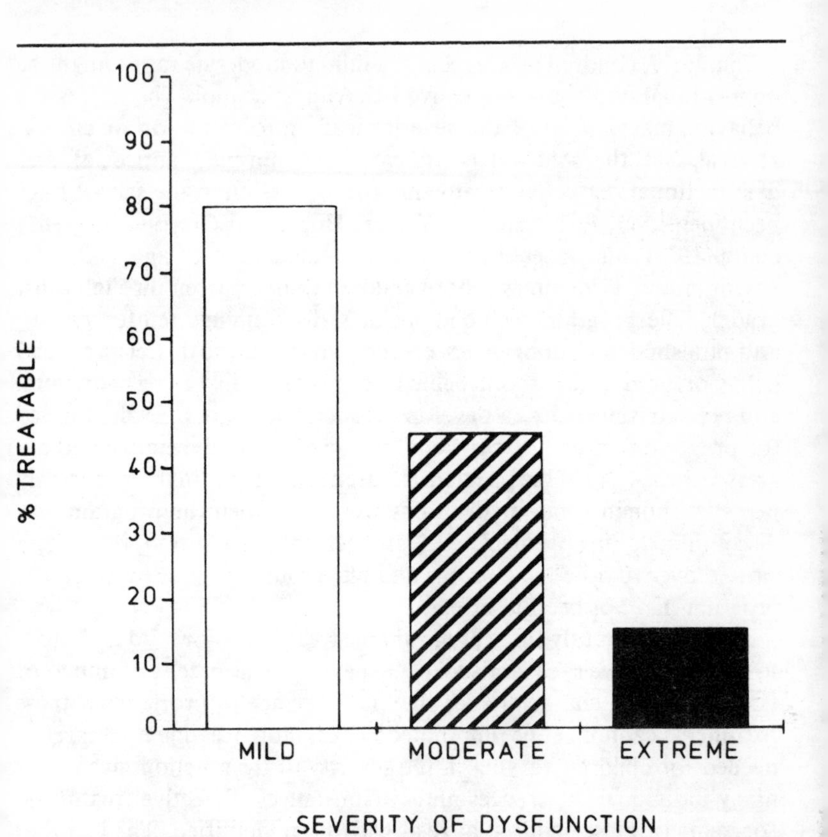

Figure 6.2 Illustration of the relative impact of currently available treatments on youths who evince different levels of severity of antisocial behavior. The information is hypothetical and reflects the percentage of youths for whom treatment might be effective.

management training for noncompliant and oppositional children (see Forehand & McMahon, 1981). The program encompasses a relatively small number of sessions (e.g., 5-12) of direct contact with the parents. The beneficial effects of the program have been well documented over the last decade (see Kazdin, 1985). There is a large group of children whose oppositional behaviors fall within the level of severity for which this program appears well suited. That level of behavior is likely to be on a continuum with those defined by a diagnosis of Conduct Disorder. The absence of clearly effective treatments for this latter group should not imply that procedures for less severely dysfunctional children and families are wanting.

Similarly, children at a level in the mild to moderate range might be oppositional and show aggressive behavior at school. The aggressive behavior may not be of the severity leading to expulsion or clinical referral. Yet, the behavior is still clearly "abnormal," antisocial, and dysfunctional. Effective treatments for aggression in the school have been identified. For example, Walker, Hops, and Greenwood (1981) conducted a multifaceted program for remediation of aggressive behavior among elementary school children (kindergarten through third grade). The program included social skills training, reinforcement, and punishment contingencies on the playground to foster prosocial behavior, and a classroom behavioral program involving individual and peer contingencies to develop prosocial behaviors. Evaluation of the program revealed that the contingencies reduced negative and aggressive behaviors of the problem children to the levels of their "normal" peers. Although some of the gains were lost when the program was discontinued, improvements were still evident. In addition, the effects carried over to other classrooms and playground periods in which the program had not been in effect.

In short, currently there are available treatments for mild and mild-to-moderate levels of antisocial behavior. The precise number of youths and the characteristics they must evince to profit from these treatments cannot yet be pinpointed. Thus, more treatment research is needed for children varying in the severity of dysfunction given their many individual differences and circumstances. Effective treatments for many of these children have already been identified. The fact that the population is only mildly antisocial should not be viewed as a retreat from the task of treating the genuinely severe youths. Research can continue on that front while the gains with less disturbed children are consolidated. Moreover, successful intervention with mildly antisocial youths may directly help the problem of clinically severe dysfunction. Mildly antisocial youths are at risk for more severe antisocial behavior. Therapeutic effects with mildly antisocial youths can be considered as secondary preventive work—that is, controlling the problem so that its course and severity are contained.

Increasing Treatment Strength

Dissemination of current treatments for a subsample of oppositional or mildly antisocial children is clearly not enough. The group with severe clinical dysfunction is not that rare to neglect the problem or to relegate it to a low priority. Also, severely antisocial children present a major social problem because of the disproportionate impact they have (e.g., in accounting for victimization of others, repeated crime, and costs to society). Conduct disorder is usually identified and treated in late childhood and early adolescence. At this point in the development, antisocial behaviors may be well entrenched. Any intervention may need to be particularly strong to exert impact and to overcome other deleterious influences (e.g., extended exposure to poor child rearing, peer pressures). An important direction to help identify effective treatments may be to increase the strength or intensity of existing treatments.

Increased intensity or dose of treatment have relatively clear meaning in the case of many medical treatments. Obviously, dose in psychopharmacology in particular has meaning given the availability of methods to assess the amount of the medication (e.g., per unit of body weight or plasma concentration). Similarly, although less well quantified, there is a continuum of intensity among alternative treatments. For a particular class of problems (e.g., low back pain, arthritis), available treatments (e.g., exercise, medication, surgery) may vary in the extent to which they are intrusive, place the patient at risk for other problems, and are considered to reflect the intensity of effort to ameliorate the problem.

For psychosocial treatments, strength, dose, and intensity of treatment are less clearly defined and hence more difficult to monitor and assess. The problem stems in part from nebulous or poor conceptualizations of treatment. To vary or increase the strength of treatment, one must have some idea regarding procedures or processes that account for therapeutic change. Only when these processes are identified and described can they be explicitly maximized in the context of treatment.

A seemingly obvious way of increasing the strength of treatment is to increase the amount of treatment in some way. For example, the number of sessions provided and their duration might be increased. Yet, those portions of treatment that produce therapeutic change may not increase linearly with extensions in duration. Perhaps crucial therapeutic processes occur at a particular point in therapy or different therapeutic practices are needed at different points in time. Simple extensions of treatment duration are conceptually wanting and should not be accorded expectations for improved efficacy without better elaboration of what is expected to change and why.

On the other hand, many treatment trials for conduct disorder children have included relatively brief and time-limited treatments. For example, in several studies of individual and group psychotherapy, behavior therapy, parent management training, and problem-solving skills therapy, treatment is administered in a period of 5-15 sessions over a period of 1-3 months. It is difficult to judge treatment duration in any absolute sense. However, one wonders if treatments of this or twice this duration might be expected on a priori grounds to be able to controvert antisocial and delinquent behavior.

An important future direction for treatment research is to consider the notion of strength of treatment in designing clinical trials. Specifically, treatments need to be implemented in such a way as to provide an optimal and/or maximal dose. The model that needs to be adopted for problems that have not responded to the usual ministrations is to aim for the *strongest feasible version* of treatment to see if the problem can be altered. If the strongest version of treatment can produce change, then it is reasonable to study whether less protracted, less costly, less difficult-to-implement procedures can achieve similar outcomes or whether any loss in treatment gain is worth the savings in cost or ease of administration.

There are problems with attempting to test the maximum strength of treatment. In the case of medical treatments, risks to the patient are recognized to limit increases of treatment strength. However, risks are often increased when there is no known effective treatment or when the failure to treat effectively itself has a predictable and fatal outcome (e.g., terminal cancer). The problems are different for psychotherapies where the side effects are less well known and typically not life threatening. Also, the dimensions that determine strength of treatment are unknown. Thus, a well-intentioned clinical researcher would not necessarily know how to maximize the strength of treatment if he or she wanted to. Expert opinion may serve as a possible basis for identifying whether a proposed intervention is likely to provide a strong test of treatment (Sechrest et al., 1979). The use of experts in this fashion might be helpful, because some current treatment trials seem to be weak tests by design. Yet opinion by itself is obviously limited. Theory underlying the treatment is also a guide, as noted already.

There are practical limits as well to increases in the strength of treatment. A critical limitation to applying treatment is what consumers (children, parents, third-party payers) will allow. The idea of protracted and intensive treatment for deviant behavior is not as familiar or probably as well accepted as protracted punishment for criminal acts. Also, with current treatments, it is often difficult to continue patients in care for extended periods. Patient attrition is one of the many problems that limits how long treatments can be implemented. However, perhaps stronger treatments may not translate simply to longer and more sessions for reasons noted above. Additional research is needed that tries to effect change with stronger treatments than have been tested. Such evaluations would provide improved tests of the extent to which current treatments can effectively alter severe conduct disorder.

ALTERNATIVE MODELS OF TREATMENT

The current advances and limitations of treatment and prevention research for antisocial children and adolescents can be used as a basis for considering entirely different models of treatment. In the usual model of treatment research, a *specific intervention* is applied to a *clinically identified group* for a *specific, time-limited duration* and *evaluated after treatment is terminated.* The limitations in what has been learned to date from the usual treatment model elevate the urgency in considering alternative models of identifying effective treatments. Three models are proposed to guide future intervention research.

Amenability to Treatment Model

The earlier comments related to the simplified classification of antisocial behavior as mild, moderate, and extreme raise one approach toward treatment trials that is not in widespread use. Consider more realistically the complexity of antisocial behavior and research completed on the characteristics of such youth and their families. From what has been learned, it is likely that youths can be identified who would vary in their responsiveness to treatments. A model for treatment research yet to be sufficiently exploited would be to identify where interventions are likely to be successful—that is, with those children who are most *amenable to treatment*. The obvious idea is to select individuals who would be highly likely to profit from treatment and then to evaluate the efficacy of the intervention in a controlled trial. Once treatments were shown to be successful, they could then be extended to less amenable cases.

Amenability to treatment can be conceived in several different ways. Severity of behavior and level of family risk factors are two candidates to help define amenability, a point noted above in the discussion of mild, moderate, and extreme antisocial behavior. Successful identification of effective outcomes with less severe cases would provide an excellent basis for extending treatments to more severe cases. If treatments did not produce change with youths considered to be less seriously disturbed or low in family and parent risk factors, the likelihood of the procedures working with more recalcitrant samples is small.

The extent to which a child is amenable to treatment may depend upon many factors other than characteristics of the antisocial behaviors. For example, children who are functioning well in areas of performance often correlated with antisocial behavior also are more likely to be amenable to treatment than those who are functioning poorly. Reading disability and academic dysfunction are commonly associated with antisocial child behavior. Quite possibly children whose academic performance is adequate may be more amenable to treatment. Whether academic performance in general or reading ability is the specific variable that makes a child more amenable to treatment is not the issue. Academic competence may reflect a larger dimension such as impact of dysfunction or personal resources that influence amenability to treatment.

There are many other characteristics of the child (e.g., age, intelligence, social competence) that might be related to amenability to treatment. Preliminary evidence attesting to the utility of the general model has been provided with a delinquent sample. Adams (1970) evaluated individual psychotherapy with institutionalized older delinquents (N = 400, age range 17-23 years) who had been randomly assigned to treatment or no-treatment control groups. Youths were delineated as "amenable" or "nonamenable" to treatment on the basis of pooled clinical judgment derived from several characteristics of the youths. Amenable youths were more intelligent, verbal, anxious, insightful, aware of their problems, and interested in change.

Treatment consisted of one or two weekly counseling sessions given for an average of 9 months. Some youths also received group therapy. After treatment and up to a 3-year follow-up, amenable youths who received treatment did significantly better than controls, as reflected in reduced recidivism. In contrast, nonamenable treated youths did worse in comparison to controls. The study points to the potential benefits of identifying youths with antisocial behavior and delineating their likely amenability to treatment.

The approach of identifying youths more or less amenable to research can be integrated into existing controlled outcome research. Within a given study, youths need to be identified as more or less amenable to the intervention based on characteristics of the sample and hypotheses about the interface of treatment and child or parent variables. Analyses of outcome effects are then based on comparisons of subgroups within the investigation to assess differential responsiveness to treatment as a function of amenability.

Broad-Based Interventions

In the typical application of treatment, a particular intervention is implemented to alter an important facet of the child and/or the system in which the child functions. The facet that is targeted is considered on theoretical or clinical grounds to be central to the child's problem. In the usual case, the focus may be relatively narrow, as evident even in such seemingly broad terms such as psychic conflict, self-esteem, cognitive processes, and behavioral repertoires. In light of the pervasiveness of the dysfunction that conduct disorder represents, the scope of most treatments may not be sufficiently broad.

For example, parent management training emphasizes the importance of parent-child interaction and its contribution to deviant child behavior. Many problems within the family (e.g., parent psychopathology and marital discord) are not usually focused on in treatment, although they may be relevant to the success and outcome for the child. Perhaps even more obvious, parent management training does not focus on the child in the sense of improving his or her coping skills and interpersonal resources. Although the conceptual model upon which parent management training is based does not emphasize the child's resources in responding to his or her own environment, there is ample evidence that such children have special problems in their own interpersonal repertoires (Dodge, 1985; Spivack et al., 1976). Treatment can be expanded to address this and other domains known to be deficient or problematic.

There is no reason to single out parent management training. Indeed, among alternative treatments, parent management training is one of the more broadly focused interventions because it encompasses home and school functioning of the child as well as family interaction patterns. Yet, currently available treatments tend to have a relatively narrow focus. Even if treatment achieved its purported goals, what could one reasonably expect? For example, if *individual psychotherapy* with a child achieved the maximum benefits for those psychological domains that are altered, could one expect less aggressive behavior, more prosocial behavior at school, improved grades, or reduced temper tantrums in response to parent belligerence? The connections between improved functioning in therapy, as defined by alternative approaches to individual psychotherapy (e.g., nondirective, psychodynamic), and changes in the many domains in which antisocial youths are deficient have not been established empirically. Similarly, for *social skills training,* a behavioral approach that focuses directly on behavior, it seems unreasonable on a priori grounds to expect changes in other domains noted here. One would hope for improved prosocial behavior. Yet, changes in other domains do not necessarily follow.

One direction for future research is to broaden the comprehensiveness or scope of interventions from their typical application to address a large set of domains relevant to the individual youth's dysfunction. Treatment may need to be conceived of in a *modular fashion* where there are separate components that are woven into an overall treatment regimen. There might be a need for focusing on separate areas of the child's dysfunction including treatment for the family (parent management training, family therapy) and the child (e.g., cognitive therapy, individual psychotherapy). In addition, different areas of the child's behavior may need to receive special treatments (e.g., medication to gain control of aggressive acts, behavior modification contingencies for the classroom and community settings).

The idea of multifaceted treatments is not at all new. Indeed, clinical researchers have long recognized the multiple problems of conduct problem children and their families and have proposed treatments that provide family casework, community mental health services, and vocational guidance, plus the usual direct treatment of child and parental dysfunction (e.g., Glick, 1972). Some treatment regimens routinely provide such diverse services. As a prime example, residential treatment programs for antisocial children often include a wide array of interventions involving virtually all of the mental health related disciplines. Indeed, accreditation requirements often dictate the participation of personnel from diverse disciplines and orientations in treatment, independently of the demonstrated efficacy of the specific interventions they provide (see Kazdin, 1985).

There are other examples of broad-based treatments in which a select number of components or modules are integrated. As an example, Massimo and Shore (1963, 1967) provided psychotherapy, vocational placement, and remedial education. Similarly, in the Cambridge-Somerville study, youths were provided with individual and family counseling, academic tutoring, contact with community programs, and psychiatric and medical attention as needed (Powers & Witmer, 1951). These studies illustrate some of the many attempts to provide comprehensive treatments, but they are *not* proposed here as models to guide future treatment research. There are difficulties with these and other studies that point to the need for fresh evaluation efforts of multifaceted treatments.

First, the different components have been provided unsystematically or on an as-needed basis. Not all persons receive all components of treatment or the same amount of a given component. Individualization of treatment is fine, but decision-rules need to be explicit so that one knows who received what treatment, when, and why. Second, treatment components are rarely described in a fashion that permit their duplication in clinical work or replication in research. Finally, treatment integrity of the different components has not been assessed in most applications of multifaceted treatments, so that there is no assurance that treatments have been tested or that individual components have been provided.

Broad-based programs tested to date have been very well intended and in fact are directed to problematic areas of dysfunction that are readily defensible. Yet, the agglomeration of techniques is often haphazard and multiple procedures are selected for their intuitive appeal and face validity. The selection of the treatments for a more comprehensive focus needs to be based upon the best available conceptualizations and evidence. For example, if parent management training, functional family therapy, and cognitively based therapy are promising, their integration may warrant serious consideration. As currently practiced, these techniques have different foci but address important and problematic facets of antisocial youths and their families. Moreover, their combination is reasonable because of outcome evidence for their individual effects and compatibility of their integration.

In general, the purpose of combining alternative treatments is to address different facets of the problem of antisocial behavior. The combination is justified on the basis of evidence that different domains are relevant to and predict future antisocial behavior *and* the absence of a clearly defined individual treatments at present that reliably ameliorate conduct disorder or controvert its long-term course. The combination requires careful consideration and conceptual justification to avoid the mere collection of techniques, each of which might be administered in a well-intentioned but highly diluted fashion. Many current treatments suffer from weak conceptual bases already. The combination of multiple techniques without regard to what they are supposed to do and how they are to be administered potentially compounds the problem.

Future research might move toward a more comprehensive approach with multiple treatment components. The approach should be guided by initial evidence that the constituent techniques produce some change and that the domain of the focus is relevant to the problem. The danger of multifaceted treatments is that at the end of the investigation one cannot identify what component(s) accounted for change. At present, the *prior danger* to be avoided is the failure to identify effective treatments. Once such a multifaceted treatment were shown to produce change, it might be quite worthwhile then to begin to analyze the contributions of individual components.

A Chronic Disease Model

The final model to be proposed as a guide to treatment research warrants some prefatory comments. There is within psychology and other social sciences, a frequently voiced disdain for the "medical model" of psychopathology or deviant behavior. The model is proposed to help explain how a particular dysfunction came about, how it should be treated, and what might occur in the future with and without treatment. Actually, there are many different models of disease, injury, and dysfunction within medicine (Buss, 1966). It is not difficult to select one of these models (e.g., bacterial infection, systemic disease, trauma) and to convey how it is patently inappropriate as a model for a particular set of deviant or normal behaviors. There is no interest here in entering into the broader discussion about medical models and the strengths and limitations of their applications within medicine or other areas (Kazdin, 1978).

One medical model among the many may prompt an important approach for the treatment of conduct disorder, namely that of chronic disease. There are of course many chronic diseases and here too one might distinguish different models based on emergence of the disease, the underlying causes, and response to treatment. Among many diseases, diabetes mellitus is relatively familiar and one that illustrates the issues that are applicable to conduct disorder. Diabetes is a disease with multiple manifestations and variations. Stated oversimply, the disease consists of the insufficient production of insulin. Characteristically, diabetes is viewed as a chronic condition that is not treated in such a fashion that it will go away. Treatment is based on the assumption that the person suffers from a condition that requires continued care, management, and treatment.

The case does not need to be made that conduct disorder and diabetes share some startling similarities to entertain the potential utility of the model that is proposed. The usual model of treatment for conduct disorders and psychosocial problems more generally is to administer a particular intervention over a period of time (e.g., weeks or months), to terminate the treatment and to hope for and/or marvel at the permanent changes. This model *is* very much like an inappropriate medical model (e.g., bacterial infection) where the antidote (i.e., antibiotics) is given and is expected to eliminate the problem. Indeed, the model would also be inappropriate for a disease like diabetes where an effective treatment (e.g., insulin) for a delimited period would not, after termination, be expected to ameliorate the problem.

It might be heuristically valuable to consider conduct disorder, at least for contemporary work, as a chronic condition that requires intervention, continued monitoring, and evaluation over the course of one's life. There are separate reasons to entertain the model seriously. First, research on conduct disorder suggests that it is very much like a chronic condition in terms of the development and course. Also, the dysfunction has broad impact both during childhood (e.g., in affecting behavior at home and at school; interpersonal, academic and cognitive spheres) and adulthood (e.g., psychological, social, and work adjustment).

Second, there are in fact a number of therapeutic procedures that can produce change in antisocial behaviors. Many behavioral treatments in particular such as social skills training and reinforcement and punishment programs have been effective in altering aggressive behavior (see Kazdin, 1985). More dramatically, comprehensive programs for antisocial youths (e.g., Achievement Place) have been extremely effective while they are implemented (Kirigin et al., 1982). Yet, these programs have as a rule shown little long-term effects after treatment is terminated. The fact that treatments can achieve marked changes while they are in effect, using the usual model, is interpreted as representing failure, that is, that the treatments are good but not good enough. Alternatively, the treatments could be viewed, within a chronic disease model, as quite effective. The treatments merely need to be applied in some form on a continuous basis.

Again, there is no need to press the analogy of diabetes and conduct disorder. However, diabetes helps to convey a very different model from the one usually implicit in studies of treatment of conduct disorder. Also, there is an interesting aspect of the treatment of diabetes that may be relevant. Treatment of diabetes has been considered to require continued administration of insulin, the model adopted here. However, current work on organ transplants suggests that there might well be a permanent cure of diabetes for many persons, although it may be premature to state within the next few years the actual effective application of the procedure. Yet, the point to underscore is that adopting a chronic disease model for treatment of conduct disorder is not a permanent commitment to this model. The model points to the need for continued care and monitoring of functioning until the time that a better, more abbreviated, and more effective intervention is developed.

General Comments

The above discussion identifies three alternative models that might be used to identify effective treatments for antisocial children. Given that so much has been attempted with antisocial youths, one might argue that each model has been repeatedly applied and cite examples that reflect close approximations. For example, prevention studies focusing on high-risk youths and community interventions that provide multiple services to behavior problem children might well be seen to reflect the *amenability to treatment* and *broad-based treatment models,* advocated above. Yet, little work has been accomplished to focus on conduct disorder, to address risk variables of known significance for long-term prognosis, to combine multiple facets of treatment in a reasoned way, and then to evaluate their subsequent impact on conduct disorder or adult functioning. In short, the models have not been applied in a way to address the issues noted here.

Similarly, the *chronic disease model,* as applied to mental health problems, is not new. There are already facets of mental health problems that are viewed in this fashion (e.g., Alcoholics Anonymous views of treatment for the alcoholic). Conduct disorder is a prime candidate for consideration because the fact that it reflects a chronic condition is already well known. A crucial feature of the model, yet to be applied, is to assess the youth's progress periodically (e.g., at home, school, and the community) to monitor the extent to which he or she is adjusting well, and to use the information to reapply treatment. Indeed, the key to treating diabetes has been the assessment of the extent to which the patient has control over blood glucose levels. Whether treatment is to be increased, decreased or altered markedly depends upon the feedback that assessment provides. Assessment of a child or adolescent's progress does not raise insurmountable problems for application of a similar model.

CLOSING COMMENTS

Many of the comments have been directed toward reconsideration of the models of conceptualizing antisocial behavior for the purposes of diagnosis and treatment. The comments have hardly been heretical given that they have endorsed fairly traditional approaches and current progress, in addition to calling for different models of diagnosis and treatment. It remains presumptuous to call for cessation of current work in an area to make room for "new and improved" approaches, even though the dramatic effect of such a call is almost irresistible to any writer. It is clear that more research and better research, the common final plea of most reviews, falls very short given the scope of the problem that antisocial behavior presents. In addition to what is currently under way, very different types of work should be encouraged to expand upon existing approaches.

Further scientific advances are likely to follow from increasingly more refined assessments, evaluations, and analyses of conduct disorder. Along with greater specificity in diagnosis, assessment, and treatment, it is critical to keep in mind broader social issues. Serious aggressive behavior comes in many forms (e.g., rape, child abuse, terrorism) and represents a problem of worldwide proportions and concern (see Goldstein, 1983; Goldstein & Segall, 1983). Within our own society there are many influences that may make reduction of conduct disorder and effective treatment of antisocial behavior particularly difficult. It is not quite fair to restrict the tasks of "curing" or "managing" antisocial behavior to the mental health and legal professions. There are many weighty social issues that touch upon antisocial behavior and its emergence in juveniles. Pervasive family violence (e.g., spouse and child abuse), violence in the media (e.g., television, movie theaters, and newscasts), school discipline practices involving corporal punishment, gun control, and many others have facets that touch on or contribute to the problem of antisocial behavior.

It would be unreasonable to claim that gains in the area of conduct disorder are unlikely without resolving the pervasive social issues related to violent and aggressive behavior. On the other hand, to view the clinical dysfunction as entirely free from sociocultural influences may be misleading as well. The present book has focused on the clinical dysfunction among children and adolescents. The range of factors that influence the emergence of conduct disorder is broad. The breadth not only suggests the complexity of the problem but also points to possible areas to intervene to produce change.

NOTES

1. There are two competing influences that detract from an approach to expand classification in the manner suggested here. The first is the approach of clinical diagnosis that focuses on problems *within* the individual. This approach is unwittingly fostered by multivariate approaches to diagnosis that bring to bear quantitative techni-

ques to better establish diagnostic entities. The focus of multivariate approaches often remains at the level of individuals and their problems. A very different influence is the view that children and families need to be considered individually and that classification by its very nature ignores individual differences. This latter view of course is anticlassification. The problem in relation to the present discussion is that both traditional diagnostic and anticlassification views unite to discourage further classification efforts that move away from the individual child.

2. The oversimplification stems from combining many different considerations such as onset of the behavior, diversity of symptoms, and situations across which they are performed into a single dimension "mild to extreme severity of antisocial behavior." Each of the different considerations could serve as a basis for defining severity.

REFERENCES

Achenbach, T. M. (1985). *Assessment and taxonomy of child and adolescent psychopathology*. Beverly Hills, CA: Sage.

Achenbach, T. M., & Edelbrock, C. S. (1981). Behavioral problems and competencies reported by parents of normal and disturbed children aged four through sixteen. *Monographs of the Society for Research in Child Development, 46* (188).

Achenbach, T. M., & Edelbrock, C. S. (1983). *Manual for the Child Behavior Checklist and Revised Child Behavior Profile*. Burlington, VT: University Associates in Psychiatry.

Adams, S. (1970). The PICO Project. In N. Johnston, L. Savitz, & M. E. Wolfgang (Eds.), *The sociology of punishment and correction*. New York: John Wiley.

Alexander, J. F. (1973). Defensive and supportive communications in normal and deviant families. *Journal of Consulting and Clinical Psychology, 40*, 223-231.

Alexander, J. F., Barton, C., Schiavo, R. S., & Parsons, B. V. (1976). Systems-behavioral intervention with families of delinquents: Therapist characteristics, family behavior, and outcome. *Journal of Consulting and Clinical Psychology, 44*, 656-664.

Alexander, J. F., & Parsons, B. V. (1973). Short-term behavioral intervention with delinquent families: Impact on family process and recidivism. *Journal of Abnormal Psychology, 81*, 219-225.

Alexander, J. F., & Parsons, B. V. (1982). *Functional family therapy*. Monterey, CA: Brooks/Cole.

American Psychiatric Association. (1980). *Diagnostic and statistical manual of mental disorders* (3rd ed.). Washington, DC: Author.

American Psychiatric Association. (1980). *DSM-III-R in Development* (Draft—10/5/85). Washington, DC: Author.

Arbuthnot, J., & Gordon, D. A. (1986). Behavioral and cognitive effects of a moral reasoning development intervention for high-risk behavior-disordered adolescents. *Journal of Consulting and Clinical Psychology, 54*, 208-216.

Bachman, J. G., Johnston, L. D., & O'Malley, P. M. (1978). Delinquent behavior linked to educational attainment and post-high school experiences. In L. Otten (Ed.), *Colloquium on the correlates of crime and the determinants of criminal behavior*. Arlington, VA: The MITRE Corp.

Barton, C., & Alexander, J. F. (1981). Functional family therapy. In A.S. Gurman & D. P. Kniskern (Eds.), *Handbook of family therapy*. New York: Brunner/Mazel.

Baum, C. G., & Forehand, R. (1981). Long-term follow-up assessment of parent training by use of multiple outcome measures. *Behavior Therapy, 12*, 643-652.

Beach, C. F., & Laird, J. D. (1968). Follow-up study of children identified early as emotionally disturbed. *Journal of Consulting and Clinical Psychology, 32*, 369-374.

Behar, D., & Stewart, M. A. (1982). Aggressive conduct disorder of children. *Acta Psychiatrica Scandinavica, 65*, 210-220.

Berkowitz, L. (1977). Situational and personal conditions governing reactions to aggressive cues. In D. Magnusson & N. S. Endler (Eds.), *Personality at the crossroads: Current issues in interactional psychology*. Hillsdale, NJ: Erlbaum.

Bien, N. Z., & Bry, B. H. (1980). An experimentally designed comparison of four intensities of school-based prevention programs for adolescents with adjustment problems. *Journal of Community Psychology, 8,* 110-116.

Blashfield, R. K. (1984). *The classification of psychopathology: Neo-Kraepelinian and quantitative approaches.* New York: Plenum.

Block, J. (1978). Effects of rational-emotive mental health program on poorly achieving, disruptive high school students. *Journal of Consulting Psychology, 25,* 61-65.

Brown, L., Ebert, M. H., Goyer, P. F., Jimerson, D. C., Klein, W. J., Bunney, W. E., & Goodwin, F. K. (1982). Aggression, suicide and serotonin: Relationships to CSF amine metabolites. *American Journal of Psychiatry, 139,* 741-745.

Bry, B. H. (1982). Reducing the incidence of adolescent problems through preventive intervention: One- and five-year follow-up. *American Journal of Community Psychology, 10,* 265-276.

Bry, B. H., & George, F. E. (1980). The preventive effects of early intervention on the attendance and grades of urban adolescents. *Professional Psychology, 11,* 252-260.

Buss, A. H. (1966). *Psychopathology*. New York: John Wiley.

Cadoret, R. J. (1978). Psychopathology in adopted-away offspring of biological parents with antisocial behavior. *Archives of General Psychiatry, 35,* 176-184.

Cadoret, R. J., & Cain, C. (1980). Sex differences in predictors of antisocial behavior in adoptees. *Archives of General Psychiatry, 37,* 1171-1175.

Cadoret, R. J., & Cain, C. (1981). Environmental and genetic factors in predicting adolescent antisocial behavior. *Psychiatric Journal of the University of Ottawa, 6,* 220-225.

Cadoret, R. J., Cain, C., & Crowe, R. R. (1983). Evidence for gene-environment interaction in the development of adolescent antisocial behavior. *Behavior Genetics, 13,* 301-310.

Camp, B. W., & Bash, M. A. S. (1985) *Think aloud: Increasing social and cognitive skills—A problem-solving program for children classroom program.* Champaign, IL: Research Press.

Campbell, M., Small, A. M., Jennings, S. J., Perry, R., Bennett, W. G., & Anderson, L. (1984). Behavioral efficacy of haloperidol and lithium carbonate. *Archives of General Psychiatry, 41,* 650-656.

Carlson, C. L., Lahey, B. B., & Neeper, R. (1984). Peer assessment of the social behavior of accepted, rejected, and neglected children. *Journal of Abnormal Child Psychology, 12,* 189-198.

Chambers, W. J., Puig-Antich, J., Hirsch, M., Paez, P., Ambrosini, P. J., Tabrizi, M. A., & Davies, M. (1985). The assessment of affective disorders in children and adolescents by semistructured interview: Test-retest reliability of the K-SADS-P. *Archives of General Psychiatry, 42,* 696-702.

Chandler, C. L., Weissberg, R. P., Cowen, E. L., & Guare, J. (1984). Long-term effects of a school-based secondary prevention program for young maladapting children. *Journal of Consulting and Clinical Psychology, 52,* 165-170.

Christiansen, K. O. (1974). Seriousness of criminality and concordance among Danish twins. In R. Hood (Ed.), *Crime, criminology and public policy*. London: Heinemann.

Cloninger, C. R., Christiansen, K. O., Reich, T., & Gottesman, I. I. (1978). Implications of sex differences in the prevalences of antisocial personality, alcoholism, and criminality for familial transmission. *Archives of General Psychiatry, 35,* 941-951.

Cloninger, C. R., Reich, T., & Guze, S. B. (1975). The multifactorial model of disease transmission: II. Sex differences in the familial transmission of sociopathy (antisocial personality). *British Journal of Psychiatry, 127,* 11-22.

Cloninger, C. R., Reich, T., & Guze, S. B. (1978). Genetic-environmental interactions and antisocial behaviour. In R. D. Hare & D. Schalling (Eds.), *Psychopathic behaviour: Approaches to research.* Chichester, England: John Wiley.

Cloninger, C. R., Sigvardsson, S., Bohman, M., & von Knorring, A. (1982). Predisposition to petting criminality in Swedish adoptees: II. Cross-fostering analysis of gene-environment interaction. *Archives of General Psychiatry, 39,* 1242-1247.

Cole, P. M., & Kazdin, A. E. (1980). Cricial issues in self-instruction training with children. *Child Behavior Therapy, 2,* 1-23.

Conners, C. K. (1969). A teacher rating scale for use in drug studies with children. *American Journal of Psychiatry, 126,* 884-888.

Conners, C. K. (1970). Symptom patterns in hyperkinetic, neurotic, and normal children. *Child Development, 41,* 667-682.

Cowen, E. L., Gesten, E. L., & Wilson, A. B. (1979). The Primary Mental Health Project (PMHP): Evaluation of current program effectiveness. *American Journal of Community Psychology, 7,* 293-303.

Cowen, E. L., Pederson, A., Babigan, H., Izzo, L. D., & Trost, N. (1973). Long-term follow-up of early detected vulnerable children. *Journal of Consulting and Clinical Psychology, 41,* 438-446.

Cowen, E. L., Spinell, A., Wright, S., & Weissberg, R. P. (1983). Continuing dissemination of a school-based mental health program. *Professional Psychology, 14,* 118-127.

Crowe, R. R. (1974). An adoption study of antisocial personality. *Archives of General Psychiatry, 31,* 785-791.

Crowther, J. H., Bond, L. A., & Rolf, J. E. (1981). The incidence, prevalence, and severity of behavior disorders among preschool-aged children in day care. *Journal of Abnormal Child Psychology, 9,* 23-42.

Curtiss, G., Rosenthal, R. H., Marohn, R. C., Ostrov, E., Offer, D., & Trujillo, J. (1983). Measuring delinquent behavior in inpatient treatment settings: Revision and validation of the Adolescent Antisocial Behavior Checklist. *Journal of the American Academy of Child Psychiatry, 22,* 459-466.

Dangel, R. E., & Polster, R. A. (Eds.). (1984). *Parent training: Foundations of research and practice.* New York: Guilford.

Davidson, W. S., & Wolfred, T. R. (1977). Evaluation of a community-based behavior modification program for prevention of delinquency. *Community Mental Health Journal, 13,* 296-306.

Deluty, R. H. (1979). Children's Action Tendency Scale: A self-report measure of aggressiveness, assertiveness, and submissiveness in children. *Journal of Consulting and Clinical Psychology, 47,* 1061-1071.

Dodge, K. A. (1985). Attributional bias in aggressive children. In P. C. Kendall (Ed.), *Advances in cognitive-behavioral research and therapy* (vol. 4). Orlando, FL: Academic Press.

Dumas, J. E., & Wahler, R. G. (1983). Predictors of treatment outcome in parent training: Mother insularity and socioeconomic disadvantage. *Behavioral Assessment, 5,* 301-313.

Durlak, J. A. (1980). Comparative effectiveness of behavioral and relationship group treatment in the secondary prevention of school maladjustment. *American Journal of Community Psychology, 8,* 327-339.

Earls, F. (1981). Temperament characteristics and behavioral problems in three-year-old children. *Journal of Nervous and Mental Disease, 169,* 367-387.

Edelbrock, C. S., & Achenbach, T. M. (1980). A typology of Child Behavior Profile patterns: Distribution and correlates for disturbed children aged 6-16. *Journal of Abnormal Child Psychology, 8,* 441-470.

Elliott, D. S., & Ageton, S. S. (1980). Reconciling race and class differences in self-reported and official estimates of delinquency. *American Sociological Review, 45,* 95-110.

Elliott, D. S., Knowles, B. A., & Canter, R. J. (1981). *The epidemiology of delinquent behavior and drug use among American adolescents, 1976-1978.* Progress report to NIMH. Boulder, CO: Behavior Research Institute.

Ellis, P. L. (1982). Empathy: A factor in antisocial behavior. *Journal of Abnormal Child Psychology, 10,* 123-134.

Empey, L. T. (1982). *American delinquency: Its meaning and construction.* Homewood, IL: Dorsey.

Eyberg, S. M., & Johnson, S. M. (1974). Multiple assessment of behavior modification with families: Effects on contingency contracting and order of treated problems. *Journal of Consulting and Clinical Psychology, 42,* 594-606.

Eyberg, S. M., & Robinson, E. A. (1983). Conduct problem behavior: Standardization of a behavioral rating scale with adolescents. *Journal of Clinical Child Psychology, 12,* 347-354.

Farrington, D. P. (1975). Predicting self-reported and official delinquency. In D. P. Farrington & R. Tarling (Eds.), *Prediction in criminology.* Albany State University of New York Press.

Farrington, D. P. (1978). The family backgrounds of aggressive youths. In L. A. Hersov, M. Berger, & D. Shaffer (Eds.), *Aggression and anti-social behaviour in childhood and adolescence.* Oxford: Pergamon.

Farrington, D. P. (1984). Measuring the natural history of delinquency and crime. In R. A. Glow (Eds.), *Advances in the behavioral measurement of children* (vol. 1). Greenwich, CT: JAI Press.

Feldman, R. A., Caplinger, T. E., & Wodarski, J. S. (1983). *The St. Louis conundrum: The effective treatment of antisocial youths.* Englewood Cliffs, NJ: Prentice-Hall.

Feshbach, N. (1975). Empathy in children: Some theoretical and empirical considerations. *Counseling Psychologist, 5,* 25-30.

Fire in the United States. (1978). Washington, DC: United States Fire Administration, U.S. Department of Commerce.

Fleischman, M. J. (1982). Social learning interventions for aggressive children: From the laboratory to the real world. *The Behavior Therapist, 5,* 55-58.

Fleischman, M. J., & Szykula, S. A. (1981). A community setting replication of a social learning treatment for aggressive children. *Behavior Therapy, 12,* 115-122.

Fo., W. S. O., & O'Donnell, C. R. (1974). The buddy system: Relationship and contingency conditions in a community intervention program for youth with nonprofessionals as behavior change agents. *Journal of Consulting and Clinical Psychology, 42,* 163-169.

Fo., W. S. O., & O'Donnell, C. R. (1975). The buddy system: Effect of community intervention on delinquent offenses. *Behavior Therapy, 6,* 522-524.

Forehand, R., & McMahon, R. J. (1981). *Helping the noncompliant child: A clinician's guide to parent training.* New York: Guilford.

Forehand, R., Wells, K. C., McMahon, R. J., Griest, D. L., & Rogers, T. (1982). Maternal perceptions of maladjustment in clinic-referred children: An extension of earlier research. *Journal of Behavioral Assessment, 4,* 145-151.

Freedman, B. J., Rosenthal, L., Donahoe, C. P., Schlundt, D. G., & McFall, R. (1978). A social-behavioral analysis of skills deficits in delinquent and nondelinquent adolescent boys. *Journal of Consulting and Clinical Psychology, 46,* 1448-1462.

Gaffney, L. R., & McFall, R. M. (1981). A comparison of social skills in delinquent and nondelinquent adolescent girls using a behavioral role-playing inventory. *Journal of Consulting and Clinical Psychology, 49,* 959-967.

Galloway, D. (1985). *Schools and persistent absentees.* Oxford: Pergamon.

Gersten, J. C., Langner, T. S., Eisenberg, J. G., Simcha-Fagan, D., & McCarthy, E. D. (1976). Stability in change in types of behavioral disturbances of children and adolescents. *Journal of Abnormal Child Psychology, 4,* 111-127.

Gesten, E. L., Rains, M., Rapkin, B. D., Weissberg, R. P., Flores de Apodaca, R., Cowen, E. L., & Bowen, G. (1982). Training children in social problem-solving competencies: A first and second look. *American Journal of Community Psychology, 10,* 95-115.

Gilbert, G. M. (1957). A survey of "referral problems" in metropolitan child guidance centers. *Journal of Clinical Psychology, 13,* 37-42.

Glick, S. J. (1972). Identification of predelinquents among children with school behavior problems as basis for multiservice treatment program. In S. Glueck & E. Glueck (Eds.), *Identification of predelinquents.* New York: Intercontinental Medical Book Corp.

Glidewell, J. C. (1983). Prevention: The threat and the promise. In R. D. Felner, L. A. Jason, J. N. Moritsugu, & S. S. Farber (Eds.), *Preventive psychology: Theory, research and practice.* New York: Pergamon.

Glueck, S., & Glueck, E. (1950). *Unravelling juvenile delinquency.* Cambridge, MA: Harvard University Press.

Glueck, S., & Glueck, E. (1959). *Predicting delinquency and crime.* Cambridge, MA: Harvard University Press.

Glueck, S., & Glueck, E. (1968). *Delinquents and nondelinquents in perspective.* Cambridge, MA: Harvard University Press.

Goldstein, A. (1983). *Prevention and control of aggression.* New York: Pergamon.

Goldstein, A., & Segall, M. H. (Eds.). *Aggression in global perspective.* New York: Pergamon.

Goldstein, H. S. (1984). Parental composition, supervision, and conduct problems in youths 12 to 17 years old. *Journal of the American Academy of Child Psychiatry, 23,* 679-684.

Graham, P. (1979). Epidemiological studies. In H. C. Quay & J. S. Werry (Eds.), *Psychopathological disorders of childhood* (2nd ed.). New York: John Wiley.

Gresham, F. M. (1985). Utility of cognitive-behavioral procedures for social skills training with children: A critical review. *Journal of Abnormal Child Psychology, 13,* 411-423.

Griest, D. L., Forehand, R., Rogers, T., Breiner, J., Furey, W., & Williams, C. A. (1982). Effects of parent enhancement therapy on the treatment outcome and generalization of a parent training program. *Behaviour Research and Therapy, 20,* 429-436.

Griest, D. L., & Wells, K. C. (1983). Behavioral family therapy with conduct disorders in children. *Behavior Therapy, 14,* 37-53.

Griest, D. L., Wells, K. C., & Forehand, R. (1979). An examination of predictors of maternal perceptions of maladjustment in clinic-referred children. *Journal of Abnormal Psychology, 88,* 277-281.

Group for the Advancement of Psychiatry, Committee on Child Psychiatry. (1966). *Psychopathological disorders in childhood: Theoretical considerations and a proposed classification* (vol. 6). New York: Author.

Hackler, J. C., & Hagan, J. L. (1975). Work and teaching machines as delinquency prevention tools: A four-year follow-up. *Social Science Review, 49,* 92-106.

Hamparian, D. M., Schuster, R., Dinitz, S., & Conrad, J. P. (1978). *Violent few: A study of dangerous juvenile offenders.* Lexington, MA: D. C. Heath.

Hanson, C. L., Henggeler, S. W., Haefele, W. F., & Rodick, J. D. (1984). Demographic, individual, and family relationship correlates of serious and repeated crime among adolescents and their siblings. *Journal of Consulting and Clinical Psychology, 52,* 528-538.

Hare, R. D. (1978). Psychopathy and crime. In L. Otten (Ed.), *Colloquium on the correlates of crime and the determinants of criminal behavior.* Arlington, VA: The MITRE Corp.

Herbert, M. (1978). *Conduct disorders of childhood and adolescence: A behavioural approach to assessment and treatment.* Chichester, England: John Wiley.

Herjanic, B., & Reich, W. (1982). Development of a structured psychiatric interview for children: Agreement between child and parent on individual symptoms. *Journal of Abnormal Child Psychology, 10,* 307-324.

Hetherington, E. M., Cox, M., & Cox, R. (1979). Family interaction and the social, emotional, and cognitive development of children following divorce. In V. Vaughn & T. Brazelton (Eds.), *The family: Setting priorities.* New York: Science and Medicine.

Hetherington, E. M., & Martin, B. (1979). Family interaction. In H. C. Quay & J. S. Werry (Eds.), *Psychopathological disorders of childhood* (2nd ed.). New York: John Wiley.

Hippchen, L. J. (Ed.). (1978). *Ecologic-biochemical approaches to treatment of delinquents and criminals.* New York: Van Nostrand Reinhold.

Hirschi, T., & Hindelang, M. J. (1977). Intelligence and delinquency: A revisionist view. *American Sociological Review, 42,* 571-587.

Hodges, K., McKnew, D., Cytryn, L., Stern, L., & Kline, J. (1982). The Child Assessment Schedule (CAS) diagnostic interview: A report on reliability and validity. *Journal of the American Academy of Child Psychiatry, 21,* 468-473.

Hood, R., & Sparks, R. (1970). *Key issues in criminology.* London: Weidenfeld & Nicholson.

Hsu, L. K. G., Wisner, K., Richey, E. T., & Goldstein, C. (1985). Is juvenile delinquency related to an abnormal EEG?: A study of EEG abnormalities in juvenile delinquents and adolescent psychiatric inpatients. *Journal of the American Academy of Child Psychiatry, 24,* 310-315.

Huesmann, L. R., Eron, L. D., Lefkowitz, M. M., & Walder, L. O. (1984). Stability of aggression over time and generations. *Developmental Psychology, 20,* 1120-1134.

Hutchings, B., & Mednick, S. A. (1975). Registered criminality in the adoptive and biological parent of registered male criminal adoptees. In R. R. Fieve, D. Rosenthal, & H. Brill (Eds.), *Genetic research in psychiatry.* Baltimore: Johns Hopkins University Press.

Jacobson, N. S. (1984). A component analysis of behavioral marital therapy: The relative effectiveness of behavior exchange and communication/problem-solving training. *Journal of Consulting and Clinical Psychology, 52,* 295-305.

Jesness, C. F. (1971). Comparative effectiveness of two institutional treatment programs for delinquents. *Child Care Quarterly, 1,* 119-130.

Jesness, C. F., Allison, T., McCormick, P., Wedge, R., & Young, M. (1975). *Cooperative Behavior Demonstration Project.* Sacramento: California Youth Authority.

Jessness, C. F., & Wedge, R. F. (1984). Validity of a revised Jesness Inventory I-Level classification with delinquents. *Journal of Consulting and Clinical Psychology, 52,* 997-1010.

Jessor, R., & Jessor, S. L. (1977). *Problem behavior and psychological development: A longitudinal study of youth.* New York: Academic Press.

Johnson, D. L., & Breckenridge, J. N. (1982). The Houston parent-child development center and the primary prevention of behavior problems in young children. *American Journal of Community Psychology, 10,* 305-316.

Johnston, L. D., Bachman, J. G., & O'Malley, P. M. (1982). *Student drug use, attitudes, and beliefs: National trends.* Washington, DC: National Institute of Drug Abuse.

Kazdin, A. E. (1978). *History of behavior modification: Experimental foundations of contemporary research.* Baltimore: University Park Press.

Kazdin, A. E. (1979). Situational specificity: The two-edged sword of behavorial assessment. *Behavioral Assessment, 1,* 57-75.

Kazdin, A. E. (1980). *Research design in clinical psychology.* New York: Harper & Row.

Kazdin, A. E. (1983). Psychiatric diagnosis, dimensions of dysfunction and child behavior therapy. *Behavior Therapy, 14,* 73-99.

Kazdin, A. E. (1984). *Behavior modification in applied settings* (3rd ed.). Homewood, IL: Dorsey Press.

Kazdin, A. E. (1985). *Treatment of antisocial behavior in children and adolescents.* Homewood, IL: Dorsey Press.

Kazdin, A. E. (1986). The evaluations of psychotherapy: Research design and methododology. In S. L. Garfield & A. E. Bergin (Eds.), *Handbook of psychotherapy and behavior change: An empirical analysis* (3rd ed.). New York: John Wiley.

Kazdin, A. E., & Esveldt-Dawson, K. (in press). The Interview for Antisocial Behavior: Psychometric characteristics and concurrent validity with child psychiatric inpatients. *Journal of Psychopathology and Behavioral Assessment.*

Kazdin, A. E., Esveldt-Dawson, K., Unis, A. S., & Rancurello, M. D. (1983a). Child and parent evaluations of depression and aggression in psychiatric inpatient children. *Journal of Abnormal Child Psychology, 11,* 401-413.

Kazdin, A. E., French, N. H., & Unis, A. S. (1983b). Child, mother, and father evaluations of depression in psychiatric inpatient children. *Journal of Abnormal Child Psychology, 11,* 167-180.

Kazdin, A. E., French, N. H., Unis, A. S., & Esveldt-Dawson, K. (1983c). Assessment of childhood depression: Correspondence of child and parent ratings. *Journal of the American Academy of Child Psychiatry, 22,* 157-164.

Kazdin, A. E., Rodgers, A., Colbus, D., & Siegel, T. (in press). Children's Hostility Inventory: Measurement of aggression and hostility in psychiatric inpatient children. *Journal of Clinical Child Psychology.*

Kendall, P. C., & Braswell, L. (1985). *Cognitive-behavioral therapy for impulsive children.* New York: Guilford.

Kendall, P. C., & Hollon, S. D. (Eds.). (1979). *Cognitive-behavioral interventions: Theory, research, and procedures.* New York: Academic Press.

Kenrick, D. T., & Stringfield, D. O. (1980). Personality traits and the eye of the beholder: Crossing some traditional philosophical boundaries in the search for consistency in all of the people. *Psychological Review, 87,* 88-104.

Kirigin, K. A., Braukmann, C. J., Atwater, J. D., & Wolf, M. M. (1982). An evaluation of teaching-family (Achievement Place) group homes for juvenile offenders. *Journal of Applied Behavior Analysis, 15,* 1-16.

Klein, N. C., Alexander, J. F., & Parsons, B. V. (1977). Impact of family systems intervention on recidivism and sibling delinquency: A model of primary prevention and program evaluation. *Journal of Consulting and Clinical Psychology, 45,* 469-474.

Kolko, D. J., & Kazdin, A. E. (1986). Juvenile firesetting: Conceptualizations, implications, and future directions. *Journal of Abnormal Child Psychology, 14,* 49-61.

Kulik, J. A., Stein, K. B., & Sarbin, T. R. (1968). Dimensions and patterns of adolescent behavior. *Journal of Consulting and Clinical Psychology, 32,* 375-382.

Lapouse, R., & Monk, M. A. (1958). An epidemiologic study of behavior characteristics in children. *American Journal of Public Health, 48,* 1134-1144.

Ledingham, J. E. & Schwartzman, A. E. (1984). A 3-year follow-up of aggressive and withdrawn behavior in childhood: Preliminary findings. *Journal of Abnormal Child Psychology, 12,* 157-168.

Ledingham, J. E., Younger, A., Schwartzman, A., & Bergeron, G. (1982). Agreement among teacher, peer, and self-ratings of children's aggression, withdrawal, and likability. *Journal of Abnormal Child Psychology, 10,* 363-372.

Lefkowitz, M. M., Eron, L. D., Walder, L. O., & Huesmann, L. R. (1977). *Growing up to be violent: A longitudinal study of the development of aggression.* New York: Pergamon.

Lessing, E. E., Williams, V., & Gil, E. (1982). A cluster-analytically derived typology: Feasible alternative to clinical diagnostic classification of children? *Journal of Abnormal Child Psychology, 10,* 451-482.

Lessing, E. E., Williams, V., & Revelle, W. (1981). Parallel forms of the IJR Behavior Checklist for parents, teachers, and clinicians. *Journal of Consulting and Clinical Psychology, 49,* 34-50.

Lewis, D. O. (Ed.). (1981). *Vulnerabilities to delinquency.* New York: SP Medical & Scientific Books.

Lewis, D. O., Pincus, J. H., Shanok, S. S., & Glaser, G. H. (1982). Psychomotor epilepsy and violence in a group of incarcerated adolescent boys. *American Journal of Psychiatry, 139,* 882-887.

Lewis, D. O., Shanok, S. S., Grant, M., & Ritvo, E. (1983). Homicidally aggressive young children: Neuropsychiatric and experiential correlates. *American Journal of Psychiatry, 140,* 148-153.

Lewis, D. O., Shanok, S. S., Pincus, J. H., & Glaser, G. H. (1979). Violent juvenile delinquents: Psychiatric, neurological, psychological, and abuse factors. *Journal of the American Academy of Child Psychiatry, 18,* 307-319.

Lochman, J. E., Burch, P. R., Curry, J. F., & Lampron, L. B. (1984). Treatment and generalization effects of cognitive-behavioral and goal-setting interventions with aggressive boys. *Journal of Consulting and Clinical Psychology, 52,* 915-916.

Loeber, R. (1982). The stability of antisocial and delinquent child behavior: A review. *Child Development, 53,* 1431-1446.

Loeber, R. (1985). Patterns and development of antisocial child behavior. In G. J. Whitehurst (Ed.), *Annals of child development* (vol. 2). New York: JAI Press.

Loeber, R., & Dishion, T. J. (1983). Early predictors of male delinquency: A review: *Psychological Bulletin, 94,* 68-99.

Loeber, R., & Dishion, T. J. (1984). Boys who fight at home and school: Family conditions influencing cross-setting consistency. *Journal of Consulting and Clinical Psychology, 52,* 759-768.

Loeber, R., & Schmaling, K. B. (1985a). Empirical evidence for overt and covert patterns of antisocial conduct problems: A meta-analysis. *Journal of Abnormal Child Psychology, 13,* 337-352.

Loeber, R., & Schmaling, K. B. (1985b). The utility of differentiating between mixed and pure forms of antisocial child behavior. *Journal of Abnormal Child Psychology, 13,* 315-335.

Loney, J. (1983). Research diagnostic criteria for childhood hyperactivity. In S. B. Guze, F. J. Earls, & J. E. Barrett (Eds.), *Childhood psychopathology and development.* New York: Raven Press.

Luborsky, L., & De Rubeis, R. J. (1984). The use of psychotherapy treatment manuals: A small revolution in psychotherapy research style. *Clinical Psychology Review, 4,* 5-14.

Lundman, R. J. (1984). *Prevention and control of juvenile delinquency.* New York: Oxford University Press.

MacFarlane, J. W., Allen, L., & Honzik, M. P. (1954). *A developmental study of the behavior problems of normal children between 21 months and 14 years.* Berkeley: University of California Press.

Mash, E. J., & Johnston, C. (1983). Parental perceptions of child behavior problems, parenting self-esteem, and mothers' reported stress in younger and older hyperactive and normal children. *Journal of Consulting and Clinical Psychology, 51,* 86-99.

Massimo, J., & Shore, M. F. (1963). The effectiveness of a comprehensive vocationally oriented psychotherapeutic program for adolescent delinquent boys. *American Journal of Orthopsychiatry, 33,* 634-642.

Massimo, J. L., & Shore, M. F. (1967). Comprehensive vocationally oriented psychotherapy: A new treatment technique for lower-class adolescent delinquent boys. *Psychiatry, 30,* 229-236.

Mattsson, A., Schalling, D., Olweus, D., Low, H., & Svensson, J. (1980). Plasma testosterone, aggressive behavior, and personality dimensions in young male delinquents. *Journal of the American Academy of Child Psychiatry, 19,* 476-490.

McCord, J. (1978). A thirty-year follow-up of treatment effects. *American Psychologist, 33,* 284-289.

McCord, J. (1980). Patterns of deviance. In S. B. Sells, R. Crandall, M. Roff, J. S.

Strauss, & W. Pollin (Eds.), *Human functioning in longitudinal perspective.* Baltimore: Williams & Wilkins.

McCord, W. (1982). *The psychopath and milieu therapy: A longitudinal study.* New York: Academic Press.

McCord, W., McCord, J., & Howard, A. (1961). Familial correlates of aggression in nondelinquent male children. *Journal of Abnormal and Social Psychology, 62,* 79-93.

McCord, W., McCord, J., & Zola, I. K. (1959). *Origins of crime.* New York: Columbia University Press.

McMahon, R. J., Forehand, R., & Griest, D. L. (1981). Effects of knowledge of social learning principles on enhancing treatment outcome and generalization in a parent training program. *Journal of Consulting and Clinical Psychology, 49,* 526-532.

McManus, M., Brickman, A., Alessi, N. E., & Grapentine, W. L. (1985). Neurological dysfunction in serious delinquents. *Journal of the American Academy of Child Psychiatry, 24,* 481-486.

Mednick, S. A. (1975). Autonomic nervous system recovery and psychopathology. *Scandinavian Journal of Behavior Therapy, 4,* 55-68.

Mednick, S. A. (1978). You don't need a weatherman! In L. Otten (Ed.), *Colloquim on the correlates of crime and the determinants of criminal behavior.* Arlington, VA: The MITRE Corp.

Mednick, S. A., & Christiansen, K. O. (Eds.). (1977). *Biosocial bases of criminal behavior.*New York: Gardner Press.

Mednick, S. A., & Hutchings, B. (1978). Genetic and psychophysiological factors in asocial behaviour. In R. D. Hare & D. Schalling (Eds.), *Psychopathic behaviour: Approaches to research.* Chichester, England: John Wiley.

Miller, L. C. (1972). School Behavior Checklist: An inventory of deviant behavior for elementary school children. *Journal of Consulting and Clinical Psychology, 38,* 138-144.

Miller, L. C., Hampe, E., Barrett, C., & Noble, H. (1971). Children's deviant behavior within the general population. *Journal of Consulting and Clinical Psychology, 37,* 16-22.

Mitchell, S., & Rosa, P. (1981). Boyhood behavior problems as precursors of criminality: A fifteen-year follow-up study. *Journal of Child Psychology and Psychiatry, 22,* 19-33.

Moore, D. R., Chamberlain, P., & Mukai, L. H. (1979). Children at risk for delinquency: A follow-up comparison of aggressive children and children who steal. *Journal of Abnormal Child Psychology, 7,* 345-355.

Moore, S. F., & Cole, S. O. (1978). Cognitive self-mediation training with hyperkinetic children. *Bulletin of the Psychonomic Society, 12,* 18-20.

Moreland, J. R., Schwebel, A. I., Beck, S., & Wells, R. (1982). Parents as therapists: A review of the behavior therapy parent training literature—1975 to 1981. *Behavior Modification, 6,* 250-276.

Morrison, H. L. (1978). The asocial child: A destiny of sociopathy? In W. H. Reid (Ed.), *The psychopath: A comprehensive study of antisocial disorders and behaviors.* New York: Brunner/Mazel.

Novaco, R. W. (1978). Anger and coping with stress: Cognitive behavioral intervention. In J. P. Foreyt & D. P. Rathjen (Eds.), *Cognitive behavioral therapy: Research and application.* New York: Plenum.

Nye, F. I. (1958). *Family relationships and delinquent behavior.* New York: John Wiley.

O'Donnell, C. R., Lygate, T., & Fo., W. S. O. (1979). The buddy system: Review and follow-up. *Child Behavior Therapy, 1,* 161-169.

O'Donnell, D. J. (1985). Conduct disorders. In J. M. Weiner (Ed.), *Diagnosis and psychopharmacology of childhood and adolescent disorders.* New York: John Wiley.

Offord, D. R. (1982). Family backgrounds of male and female delinquents. In J. Gunn & D. P. Farrington (Eds.), *Abnormal offenders: Delinquency and the criminal justice system.* Chichester, England: John Wiley.

Offord, D. R., & Jones, M. B. (1983). Skill development: A community intervention program for the prevention of antisocial behavior. In S. B. Guze, F. J. Earls, & J. E. Barrett (Eds.), *Childhood psychopathology and development.* New York: Raven.

Offord, D. R., Jones, M. B., Graham, A., Poushinsky, M., Stenerson, P., Stenerson, P., & Weaver, L. (1986). *Let's get moving: A skill development program for disadvantaged youths.* Ottawa, Canada: Canadian Parks and Recreation Program.

Ollendick, T. H., & Cerny, J. A. (1981). *Clinical behavior therapy with children.* New York: Plenum.

Olweus, D. (1979). Stability of aggressive reaction patterns in males: A review: *Psychological Bulletin, 86,* 852-875.

Olweus, D., Mattsson, A., Schalling, D., & Low, H. (1980). Testosterone, aggression, physical, and personality dimensions in normal adolescent males. *Psychosomatic Medicine, 42,* 253-269.

Orvaschel, H., Puig-Antich, J., Chambers, W. J., Tabrizi, M. A., & Johnson, R. (1982). Retrospective assessment of prepubertal major depression with the Kiddie-SADS-E. *Journal of the American Academy of Child Psychiatry, 21,* 392-397.

Parsons, B. V., & Alexander, J. F. (1973). Short-term family intervention: A therapy outcome study. *Journal of Consulting and Clinical Psychology, 41,* 195-201.

Patterson, G. R. (1974). Interventions for boys with conduct problems: Multiple settings, treatments, and criteria. *Journal of Consulting and Clinical Psychology, 42,* 471-481.

Patterson, G. R. (1982). *Coercive family process.* Eugene, OR: Castalia.

Patterson, G. R. (1984). Beyond technology: The next stage in the development of parent training. In L. L'Abate (Ed.), *Handbook of family psychology and psychotherapy.* Homewood, IL: Dow Jones-Irwin.

Patterson, G. R., Chamberlain, P., & Reid, J. B. (1982). A comparative evaluation of a parent-training program. *Behavior Therapy, 13,* 638-650.

Patterson, G. R., & Fleischman, M. J. (1979). Maintenance of treatment effects: Some considerations concerning family systems and follow-up data. *Behavior Therapy, 10,* 168-185.

Patterson, G. R., Reid, J. B., Jones, R. R., & Conger, R. W. (1975). *A social learning approach to family intervention* (Vol. 1). Eugene, OR: Castalia.

Patterson, V., Levene, H., & Breger, L. (1977). A one-year follow-up of two forms of brief psychotherapy. *American Journal of Psychotherapy, 31,* 76-82.

Platt, J. E., Campbell, M., Green, W. H., & Grega, D. M. (1984). Cognitive effects of lithium carbonate and haloperidol in treatment-resistance aggressive children. *Archives of General Psychiatry, 41,* 657-662.

Plomin, R. (1983). Childhood temperament. In B. B. Lahey & A. E. Kazdin (Eds.), *Advances in clinical child psychology.* New York: Plenum.

Powers, E., & Witmer, H. (1951). *An experiment in the prevention of delinquency: The Cambridge-Sommerville Youth Study.* New York: Columbia University Press.

Prinz, R., Connor, P., & Wilson, C. (1981). Hyperactive and aggressive behaviors in childhood: Intertwined dimensions. *Journal of Abnormal Child Psychology, 9,* 191-202.

Quay, H. C. (1964). Personality dimensions in delinquent males as inferred from the factor analysis of behavior ratings. *Journal of Research in Crime and Delinquency, 1,* 33-37.

Quay, H. C. (1977). Measuring dimensions of deviant behavior: The Behavior Problem Checklist. *Journal of Abnormal Child Psychology, 5,* 227-287.

Quay, H. C. (1979). Classification. In H. C. Quay & J. S. Werry (Eds.), *Psychopathological disorders of childhood* (2nd ed.). New York: John Wiley.

Quay, H. C. (1986). A critical analysis of DSM-III as a taxonomy of psychopathology in childhood and adolescence. In T. Millon & G. Klerman (Eds.), *Contemporary directions in psychopathology.* New York: Guilford.

Rapoport, J. L., & Ismond, D. R. (1984). *DSM-III training guide for diagnosis of childhood disorders.* New York: Brunner/Mazel.

Reid, J. B. (Ed.). (1978). *A social learning approach to family intervention. Volume 2: Observation in home settings.* Eugene, OR: Castalia.

Reid, J. B., & Hendriks, A. F. C. J. (1973). Preliminary analysis of the effectiveness of direct home intervention for the treatment of predelinquent boys who steal. In L. A. Hamerlynck, L. C. Handy, & E. J. Mash (Eds.), *Behavior change: Methodology, concepts and practice.* Champaign, IL: Research Press.

Reitsma-Street, M., Offord, D. R., & Finch, T. (1985). Pairs of same-sexed siblings discordant for antisocial behavior. *British Journal of Psychiatry, 146,* 415-423.

Rickel, A. U., Dyhdalo, L. L., & Smith, R. L. (1984). Prevention with preschoolers. In M. C. Roberts & L. Peterson (Eds.), *Prevention of problems in childhood: Psychological research and applications.* New York: John Wiley.

Rickel, A. U., & Lampi, L. A. (1981). A two-year follow-up study of a preventive mental health program for preschoolers. *Journal of Abnormal Child Psychology, 11,* 15-28.

Roberts, M. C., & Peterson, L. (Eds.). (1984). *Prevention of problems in childhood: Psychological research and applications.* New York: John Wiley.

Robins, L. N. (1966). *Deviant children grown up.* Baltimore: Williams & Wilkins.

Robins, L. N. (1978). Sturdy childhood predictors of adult antisocial behavior: Replications from longitudinal studies. *Psychological Medicine, 8,* 611-622.

Robins, L. N. (1981). Epidemiological approaches to natural history research: Antisocial disorders in children. *Journal of the American Academy of Child Psychiatry, 20,* 566-680.

Robins, L. N., & Ratcliff, K. S. (1979). Risk factors in the continuation of childhood antisocial behavior into adulthood. *International Journal of Mental Health, 7,* 96-116.

Robins, L. N., West, P. A., & Herjanic, B. (1975). Arrests and delinquency in two generations: A study of black urban families and their children. *Journal of Child Psychology and Psychiatry, 16,* 125-140.

Robinson, E. A., Eyberg, S. M., & Ross, A. W. (1980). The standardization of an inventory of child conduct problem behaviors. *Journal of Clinical Child Psychology, 9,* 22-28.

Rogeness, G. A., Hernandez, J. M., Macedo, C. A., & Mitchell, E. L. (1982). Biochemical differences in children with conduct disorder socialized and undersocialized. *American Journal of Psychiatry, 139,* 307-311.

Rolf, J. E. (1972). The social and academic competence of children vulnerable to schizophrenia and other behavior pathologies. *Journal of Abnormal Psychology, 80,* 225-243.

Rutter, M. (1972). *Maternal deprivation reassessed.* Harmondsworth, England: Penguin.

Rutter, M. (1981). Psychological sequelae of brain damage in childhood. *American Journal of Psychiatry, 138,* 533-1544.

Rutter, M., Birch, H. G., Thomas, A., & Chess, S. (1964). Temperamental characteristics in infancy and the later development of behavioral disorders. *British Journal of Psychiatry, 110,* 651-661.

Rutter, M., Cox, A., Tupling, C., Berger, M., & Yule, W. (1975). Attainment and adjustment in two geographical areas. I—The prevalence of psychiatric disorder. *British Journal of Psychiatry, 126,* 493-509.

Rutter, M., & Giller, H. (1983). *Juvenile delinquency: Trends and perspectives:* New York: Penguin.

Rutter, M., Maughan, B., Mortimore, P., & Ouston, J. (1979). *Fifteen thousand hours: Secondary schools and their effects on children.* Cambridge, MA: Harvard University Press.

Rutter, M., Tizard, J., & Whitmore, K. (Eds.). (1970). *Education, health and behaviour.* London: Longmans.

Schaefer, C. E., Briesmeister, J. M., & Fitton, M. E. (Eds.). (1984). *Family therapy techniques for problem behaviors of children and teenagers.* San Francisco: Jossey-Bass.

Sears, R. R., Maccoby, E., & Levin, H. (1957). *Patterns of child rearing.* New York: Harper & Row.

Sechrest, L., White, S. O., & Brown, E. D. (1979). *The rehabilitation of criminal offenders: Problems and prospects.* Washington, DC: National Academy of Sciences.

Shaffer, D., Meyer-Bahlburg, H. F. L., & Stokman, C. L. J. (1981). The development of aggression. In M. Rutter (Ed.), *Scientific foundations of developmental psychiatry.* Baltimore: University Park Press.

Shamsie, S. J. (1981). Antisocial adolescents: Our treatments do not work—where do we go from here? *Canadian Journal of Psychiatry, 26,* 357-364.

Shanok, S. S., & Lewis, D. O. (1981). Medical histories of female delinquents: Clinical and epidemiological findings. *Archives of General Psychiatry, 38,* 211-213.

Shure, M. B., & Spivack, G. (1978). *Problem-solving techniques in child-rearing.* San Francisco: Jossey-Bass.

Shure, M. B., & Spivack, G. (1982). Interpersonal problem-solving in young children: A cognitive approach to prevention. *American Journal of Community Psychology, 10,* 341-356.

Spivack, G., Platt, J. J., & Shure, M. B. (1976). *The problem-solving approach to adjustment.* San Francisco: Jossey-Bass.

Spivack, G., & Shure, M. B. (1982). The cognition of social adjustment: Interpersonal cognitive problem-solving thinking. In B. B. Lahey & A. E. Kazdin (Eds.), *Advances in clinical child psychology* (vol. 5). New York: Plenum.

Stein, D. M., & Polyson, J. (1984). The Primary Mental Health Project reconsidered. *Journal of Consulting and Clinical Psychology, 52,* 940-945.

Stewart, M. A., DeBlois, C. S., Meardon, J., & Cummings, C. (1980). Aggressive conduct disorder children. *Journal of Nervous and Mental Disease, 168,* 604-610.

Strain, P. S., Young, C. C., & Horowitz, J. (1981). Generalized behavior change during oppositional child training: An examination of child and family demographic variables. *Behavior Modification, 5*, 15-26.

Sturge, C. (1982). Reading retardation and antisocial behaviour. *Journal of Child Psychology and Psychiatry, 23,* 21-31.

Thomas, A., & Chess, S. (1977). *Temperament and development.* New York: Brunner/Mazel.

Twito, T. J., & Stewart, M. A. (1982). A half-sibling study of aggressive conduct disorder: Prevalence of disorders in parents, brothers and sisters. *Neuropsychobiology, 8,* 144-150.

United States Senate Judiciary Committee. Subcommittee to Investigate Juvenile Delinquency (1976). *School violence and vandalism: The nature, extent and cost of violence and vandalism in the nation's schools.* Washington, DC: U.S. Government Printing office.

Virkkunen, M. (1983). Serum cholesterol levels in homicidal offenders. *Neuropsychobiology, 10,* 65-69.

Virkkunen, M., & Penttinen, H. (1984). Serum cholesterol in aggressive conduct disorder: A preliminary study. *Biological Psychiatry, 19,* 435-439.

Wadsworth, M. (1979). *Roots of delinquency: Infancy, adolescence and crime.* New York: Barnes & Noble.

Wahler, R. G., & Fox, J. J. (1980). Solitary toy play and time out: A family treatment package for children with aggressive and oppositional behavior. *Journal of Applied Behavior Analysis, 13,* 23-39.

Walker, H. M., Hops, H., & Greenwood, C. R. (1981). RECESS: Research and development of a behavior management package for remediating social aggression in the school setting. In P. S. Strain (Ed.), *The utilization of classroom peers as behavior change agents.* New York: Plenum.

Walter, H. I., & Gilmore, S. K. (1973). Placebo versus social learning effects in parent training procedures designed to alter the behavior of aggressive boys. *Behavior Therapy, 4,* 361-377.

Webster-Stratton, C., & Eyberg, S. M. (1982). Child temperament: Relationship with child behavior problems and parent-child interactions. *Journal of Clinical Child Psychology, 11,* 123-129.

Weissberg, R. P., Cowen, E. L., Lotyczewski, B. S., & Gesten, E. L. (1983). The primary mental health project: seven consecutive years of program outcome research. *Journal of Consulting and Clinical Psychology, 51*, 100-107.

Weissberg, R. P., & Gesten, E. L. (1982). Considerations for developing effective school-based social problem-solving (SPS) training programs. *School Psychology Review, 11,* 56-63.

Weissberg, R. P., Gesten, E. L., Carnike, C. L., Toro, P. A., Rapkin, B. D., Davidson, E., & Cowen, E. L. (1981). Social problem-solving skills training: A competence-building intervention with second- to fourth-grade children. *American Journal of Community Psychology, 9,* 411-423.

Wells, K. C., Forehand, R., & Griest, D. L. (1980). Generality of treatment effects from treated to untreated behaviors resulting from a parent training program. *Journal of Clinical Child Psychology, 9,* 217-219.

Wenar, C. (1984). Commentary: Progress and problems in the cognitive approach to clinical child psychology. *Journal of Consulting and Clinical Psychology, 52,* 57-62.

Werry, J. S., & Quay, H. C. (1971). The prevalence of behavior symptoms in younger elementary school children. *American Journal of Orthopsychiatry, 41,* 136-143.

West, D. J. (1967). *The young offender.* London: Duckworth.

West, D. J. (1982). *Delinquency: Its roots, careers and prospects.* Cambridge, MA: Harvard University Press.

West, D. J., & Farrington, D. P. (1973). *Who becomes delinquent?* London: Heinemann.

Williams, J. R., & Gold, M. (1972). From delinquent behavior to official delinquency. *Social Problems, 20,* 209-229.

Wilson, H. (1980). Parental supervision: A neglected aspect of delinquency. *British Journal of Criminology, 20,* 203-235.

Wiltz, N. A., & Patterson, G. R. (1974). An evaluation of parent training procedures designed to alter inappropriate aggressive behavior of boys. *Behavior Therapy, 5,* 215-211.

Winett, R. A., Stefanek, M., & Riley, A. W. (1983). Preventive strategies with children and families: Groups, organizations, communities. In T. H. Ollendick & M. Hersen (Eds.), *Handbook of child psychopathology.* New York: Plenum.

Wirt, R. D., Lachar, D., Klinedinst, J. K., & Seat, P. D. (1977). *Multidimensional description of child personality: A manual for the Personality Inventory for Children.* Los Angeles: Western Psychological Services.

Wodarski, J. S., Filipczak, J., McCombs, D., Koustenis, G., & Rusiklo, S. (1979). Follow-up on behavioral intervention with troublesome adolescents *Journal of Behavior Therapy and Experimental Psychiatry, 10,* 181-188.

Wolfgang, M. E., Figlio, R., & Sellin, T. (1972). *Delinquency in a birth cohort.* Chicago: University of Chicago Press.

Wolkind, S., & Rutter, M. (1973). Children who have been "in care"—An epidemiological study. *Journal of Child Psychology and Psychiatry, 14,* 97-105.

World Health Organization. (1978). *Mental disorders: Glossary and guide to their classification in accordance with the 9th revision of the International Classification of Diseases.* Geneva: Author.

Wright, W. E., & Dixon, M. C. (1977). Community prevention and treatment of juvenile delinquency: A review of evaluation studies. *Journal of Research in Crime and Delinquency, 14,* 35-67.

Yeaton, W. H., & Sechrest, L. (1981). Critical dimensions in the choice and maintenance of successful treatments: Strength, integrity, and effectiveness. *Journal of Consulting and Clinical Psychology, 49,* 156-167.

NAME INDEX

SUBJECT INDEX

ABOUT THE AUTHOR

Alan E. Kazdin is Professor of Child Psychiatry and Psychology at the University of Pittsburgh School of Medicine and Research Director of the Child Psychiatric Treatment Service of Western Psychiatric Institute and Clinic. He received his Ph.D. from Northwestern University and taught at The Pennsylvania State University before coming to the University of Pittsburgh. He has been a fellow at the Center for Advanced Study in the Behavioral Sciences at Stanford, president of the Association for the Advancement of Behavior Therapy, and editor of *Behavior Therapy*. Currently he is editor of the *Journal of Consulting and Clinical Psychology* and co-editor (with Benjamin Lahey) of the annual series, *Advances in Clinical Child Psychology*. Other books include *Treatment of Antisocial Behavior in Children and Adolescents, Research Design in Clinical Psychology, Behavior Modification in Applied Settings, Single-Case Research Designs, History of Behavior Modificiation,* and *The Token Economy.*

About the series . . .

Series Editor: Alan E. Kazdin, *Western Psychiatric Institute*

The Sage series in **Developmental Clinical Psychology and Psychiatry** is uniqu designed to serve several needs of the field. While the primary focus is on childh psychopathology, the series also offers monographs prepared by experts in clinical ch psychology, child psychiatry, child development, and related disciplines. The scope of series is necessarily broad because of the working assumption, if not demonstrated f that understanding, identifying, and treating problems of youth regrettably cannot accomplished by narrow, single-discipline, and parochial conceptual views. Thus series draws upon multiple disciplines and diverse views within a given discipline.

The task for individual contributors is to present the latest theory and research on vari topics, including specific types of dysfunction. Authors are asked to bridge potential the and research, research and clinical practice, and current status and future directions. T editor has recruited leaders in the field who have translated their recognized scholars and expertise into highly readable works on contemporary topics.

In this series . . .

1: CHILD DEVELOPMENT AND PSYCHOPATHOLOGY
by Donna M. Gelfand and Lizette Peterson

2: CHILD AND ADOLESCENT PSYCHOPHARMACOLOGY
by Magda Campbell, Wayne H. Green, and Stephen I. Deutsch

3: ASSESSMENT AND TAXONOMY OF CHILD AND ADOLESCENT PSYCHOPATHOLOGY
by Thomas M. Achenbach

4: INFANT PSYCHIATRY
by Klaus Minde and Regina Minde

5: SUICIDE AND ATTEMPTED SUICIDE AMONG CHILDREN AND ADOLESCENTS
by Keith Hawton

6: PSYCHOPATHOLOGY AMONG MENTALLY RETARDED CHILDREN AND ADOLESCENTS
by Johnny L. Matson and Cynthia L. Frame

7: HYPERKINETIC CHILDREN
by C. Keith Conners and Karen C. Wells

8: LIFE EVENTS AS STRESSORS IN CHILDHOOD AND ADOLESCENCE
by James H. Johnson

9: CONDUCT DISORDERS IN CHILDHOOD AND ADOLESCENCE
by Alan E. Kazdin

SAGE PUBLICATIONS
The Publishers of Professional Social Science
Newbury Park Beverly Hills London New Delhi